THIRD WORLD CONUNDRUM

A call to Christian Partnership

Max Peberdy

Exeter
The Paternoster Press

AUSTRALIA
*Bookhouse Australia Ltd
P.O. Box 115, Flemington Markets
N.S.W. 2129.*

SOUTH AFRICA
*Oxford University Press
P.O. Box 1141, Cape Town.*

British Library Cataloguing and Publication Data
Peberdy, Max
Third World Conundrum
1. Developing countries – social conditions
I Title
361.6'1'091724 HN980

ISBN 0-85364-463-2

*Typesetting and design by
New Internationalist Publications, Oxford
and printed for the Paternoster Press
Paternoster House, 3 Mount Radford Crescent
Exeter, Devon by A. Wheaton & Co. Ltd., Exeter*

CONTENTS

Foreword

Acknowledgements

Introduction

FOREWORD

This book is well-timed. Over the last two years we have witnessed a magnificent surge of generosity. Millions of pounds have been raised and spent to help the poor of the world. Now we must press on from where Band Aid and Live Aid and 'Sir' Bob felt they had to leave off. Generosity must be matched with greater understanding.

Money can help feed starving people today, but badly spent it can easily fail to put an end to the causes of their misery. They could well face hunger and death again tomorrow. Max Peberdy tells us why, and one great merit of his book is that he does so in a straightforward, readable way, drawing on a wealth of first-hand experience.

You have probably opened it because you would like to add to your own understanding; or perhaps you are educators, in the business of helping others to understand and find out what they can do. All I can say is 'read on'. A good deal of the information you need is here.

Famine has little to do with the inadequacy of Third World people. It has a good deal to do with the unjust arrangements we, and to some extent they, have made for living together in the world. Putting an end to it will not be by way of charitable hand outs. We need a strategy that strengthens local communities to help themselves. We need a partnership which acknowledges our need to receive as well as to give and that we all have riches to share. We need to accept that the problem of poverty lies as much with 'us' as with 'them'.

Somewhere near to the heart of the 'conundrum' is the word 'power'. If we've got it and we believe it is in our interest to hang on to it, we're not likely to give it up. If we really want to change the lot of those who are poor, principally, because they are powerless we must increasingly make sure that they can stand up to us instead of being patronised and pushed around.

Max Peberdy's general line of argument, which returns again and again to key words like 'power' and 'structures' is not a popular one. Some regard it as 'too political'; others, more honestly perhaps, as politics of the wrong flavour. This book, with its fund of stories, amply demonstrates that 'politics' has a human face and is just as humanitarian as other less threatening ways of relieving suffering.

The author speaks of a conundrum or puzzle. He does much to enlighten us but he will not claim to have resolved it entirely; who can? There remains for example a good deal of puzzlement as to which economic and social systems will really work, even with the best will in the world, to make them equitable. Humanity has been experimenting with society, learning how to live together, since time began. We are still strangely at a loss.

For Christians there remains a puzzle as to why tragedies such as the Ethiopia famine recur, and it is not entirely resolved by talk about personal or even systematised sin, as if it were all our fault one way or another and had little to do with the creation of a world which seems so well designed to bring out the worst in us as well as the best. And there is a puzzle, which I myself find hard to live with, as to how much progress we can expect to make. That the poor are always with us seems all too true, but what does it say about our Christian hope?

Maybe one practical expression of that hope is to work away at the world's suffering with patience, intelligence and persistence, not laying claim to all the answers, but trying to be true to what measure of understanding we have. Such, I believe, is the quiet spirit in which this book is written.

Reverend Michael Taylor
Director, Christian Aid

ACKNOWLEDGEMENTS

I owe special thanks to Christian Aid; without its support and encouragement I would not have had the opportunities to visit development projects in Africa and Asia and to see for myself the changes voluntary agencies are supporting.

I greatly appreciate the contribution made by Suzanne Garnett, David Morgan, Alyson Peberdy, Robert Pearce, and Charles Worth in discussing with me the issues raised in this book. Their comments and criticisms have proved invaluable. I would also like to thank David Howell and Heather Trenaman for so gallantly coping with my handwriting and producing numerous typed drafts.

I am also indebted to the photographic librarians at Christian Aid and the New Internationalist for allowing me to use a number of their photographs.

Finally, the greatest debt I owe is to those in Africa, Asia and Latin America, whom I describe as 'partners'. Their courage and determination to build a new society should be an inspiration to us in Britain. The best way I can repay this debt is to share with others some of the things I have experienced.

INTRODUCTION

The Third World is a puzzle – a riddle, a conundrum. We are shocked by the deaths of thousands in Ethiopia and Sudan, and saddened by the quiet suffering of millions in Asia. How can it happen that disaster and poverty occur on this scale? Are they inevitable natural phenomena or is it that Third World countries, like the Prodigal Son, have wasted their inheritance? Who or what has gone wrong?

Among Christians and non-Christians alike the response to these questions is mixed. Some shrug their shoulders and say: 'It's not our problem, and besides, any help we give is only so many drops in the ocean.'

Others believe that people with skin a different colour from ours seem to have difficulty managing their own affairs but that Christian charity demands we offer relief in an attempt to bale them out of trouble. Yet another response is from those who are uncertain as to the causes of poverty, but who nevertheless are sure that Christ expects us to seek ways to prevent such a horror as the famine in Ethiopia occurring again.

Which, if any, of these is your reaction? As you have opened this book it is unlikely to be the first, but what of the other two?

The view we hold depends on our analysis of how the world ticks. If we believe that except for nature's occasional perversity, it runs in a fair way, then poverty can be explained only by the reluctance of the poor to pull up their socks and get on with the business of wealth creation. If on the other hand we think that misery on this scale is not due to the incompetence of a thousand million individuals, our explanation centres on the forces and structures within society that maintain poverty.

The 'Years of Compassion' might well be the name of 1985 and 1986 – we jogged, sang, drank and ate our way through sponsored fun-runs, pop concerts and hunger lunches to raise money for the starving. Our imagination and concern had been captured; it was a marvellous effort, and one which drew support from all ages and groups in the country. But what now? Do we simply shelve that compasssion for another five or ten years until the next famine, and then look surprised and say, 'But we've been here before'? Or do we build on that public concern and seek ways to bring long-term solutions to human suffering?

In the past our charity has too readily side-stepped the question of *why* the poor are poor; we have conveniently ignored the central biblical call for justice and right relationships between communities and nations. But looking into the puzzle presents us with a challenge, for the kind of structures keeping millions at the margin of existence in the Third World are also present in our own society. To hold out a hand to those 'over there', is to demand action 'over here'.

If 1985 and 1986 were the years of compassion, they were also the years of patronage. There is a fine line between responding to Christ's call to love one another and using our generosity and material well-being to demonstrate superiority. To see Europeans in the famine areas working on refugee camps, treating the sick, and transporting grain, was necessary to evoke our interest and show that our efforts were making a difference, but few of the accounts ever went further to say what Africans were doing to help themselves. As a result the public is now convinced that the only hope for the rest of the world is for them to adopt our know-how and determination.

Is this the true picture? The compassion of patrons can become the compassion of partners. Those in the Third World have much to offer. Found among the most materially deprived are men and women whose Christian witness we can hardly begin to grasp. There are tremendous signs of hope if we are prepared to look. Thousands of committed individuals and organisations are working to bring about change; not only working but achieving success – it is their stories that need to be heard.

The Third World is a puzzle

Photo : Kirsty Wright – REST

Chapter One

Puzzles and Perception

A candlestick, chalice, a vase . . . or two faces? As a child I was intrigued by optical illusion games. I particularly liked drawings which showed an immediately obvious picture, but also contained a hidden image: not just a candlestick but also the profile of two men, not just a prancing horse in a meadow but a bridge over a river. Sometimes I could spot the other image, but frequently it needed to be pointed out and then with a flash – I could almost hear the click in my head – the other picture became obvious. Afterwards the new image was always easy to discover though it often became difficult to see the original.

When it comes to the people of Africa, Asia and Latin America television and the press also present us with an immediately obvious image. It consists of the starving black child, columns of refugees walking across arid landscapes, rioters in an African township, and earthquake victims being pulled from the wreckage of a house.

The image is clear – the Third World is a problem.

We Look into the Puzzle

The horrors of Ethiopia have reached into all our homes. We saw the shrunken-limbed children with vacant eyes, and were moved to tears by mothers clutching the rag-covered bodies of their dead babies. And we responded, responded with a tremendous generosity. Old people, teenagers, school-children, those who had never given a thought to either Africa or its inhabitants, jogged their way on sponsored marathons, held coffee mornings and even mortgaged their houses to raise money for the starving. Charities such as Oxfam, Christian Aid, and Save the Chidren saw their incomes double while daring and innovative organisers of Band Aid, Live Aid, Fashion Aid,

Food Aid, Art Aid and Sport Aid pushed the money collected to more than £100 million. The Third World had a problem but the media were able to evoke our compassion. It was shock treatment but it worked.

The public can be excused for thinking that the famine in Ethiopia was similar to an aeroplane disaster. Suddenly seven million people were faced by death – one day they were all right, the next disaster had struck. But it wasn't like that. The drought had been developing for three or four years before it became headline news. Both the international charities and the Ethiopian Government had tried to warn the world that it was coming but few listened until Michael Buerk and the BBC's 9 O'Clock News shocked us into action. It was as if the situation had no reality until it was shown on television and only then did it have an existence.

But what of the tragedies that have not been brought into our homes and therefore do not have this 'existence'? What of the daily Ethiopian disasters that are taking place in other parts of the globe? It is estimated that a million people died in the northern provinces of Ethiopia during 1985. Even this figure is beyond our comprehension, but throughout the world there are almost a thousand million people living at the margin of existence; each day and every day countless thousands of children die because of poverty. Their deaths are not dramatic, they do not make good television footage, and there are no cameramen sitting alongside each of these children waiting to photograph the victim's last breath. For a thousand million theirs is the quiet violence of hunger, of never having enough to eat, of being old at forty and dead at forty-five.

We have been shown the drama of poverty – when it erupts into something so obviously visible as a famine – but we have not been shown the pathways that led to the disaster, the years of history, the neglect and injustices which are the parents and grandparents of this suffering. Worse still, the picture is made more partial because the medium of television, especially television news, only deals with simple messages. Thus in the 1985 famine the message had only two strands:

Black people are starving:

white people can save them.

The coverage did good in so far as it prodded us into concern and action, but because of the simplicity of the message it has also done tremendous harm.

A little while ago I was visiting a primary school and asked a class of eight year olds to name a country other than Britain.

'Ethiopia,' said a small girl.

'And what do you know about that country?'

'They're all starving.'

'All of them?'

'Yes, all of them.'

'Can't they buy food?'

'No, they don't have any shops.'

'And what else do you know?'

'Well lots of English people have gone to help them.'

Think back to the television and newspaper accounts. Nearly all the stories pivoted around a European – a young nurse from Kent mixing a baby's feed, a volunteer doctor advising on the sanitation of a refugee camp, and RAF pilots working around the clock to transport grain. Virtually the only Africans in the pictures were those waiting to be helped. So 'white' was equated with action, and the stereotypes of Africans as poor, passive and pathetic was reinforced.

Were the Ethiopians simply waiting for us to get them out of trouble? Of course not. In fact, in some provinces all the relief and development work was being done by local people with not a European in sight. Perhaps it was necessary to show British people out there helping in order to gain our attention, but it is a narrow line between evoking compassion and embarking on an ego trip, and at times we stepped over the border.

We use the term 'Third World' as short-hand for the peoples of Africa, Latin America and Asia, but in so doing we lump the majority of the world's population into a box marked 'them' and attach suitable labels such as 'backward', 'fatalistic' and 'lacking motivation'. These 'non-us' people are by definition inferior: at worst they are portrayed as dehumanised victims of their own inadequacy; at best we find their strange customs and beliefs interesting curiosities.

This way of looking at the world is not new. It is not so long since at school we were taught that before the Romans came to Britain, it was inhabited by a barbarian people who decorated themselves in woad and lived in caves. The fact that the Bronze Age culture 2,000 years before Christ had built mathematically

Grain distribution in the famine area of northern Ethiopia. In some areas all the relief and development work is done by local people with not a European in sight.

Photo : Kirsty Wright – REST

precise observatories such as Stonehenge, constructed burial sites on the scale of Silbury Hill and had trade routes that reached across Europe, was not considered. Similarly our lessons about other countries were confined to drawing igloos and collecting labels from tea packets. We did not learn, perhaps our teachers did not know, about the cultures which made the sixteenth-century bronzes of West Africa, or the sophisticated empires which ruled the Sahel until the slave traders arrived, or the civilisation that existed in Zimbabwe before colonisation. No, Africa and Asia were places of darkness where the European brought light.

Why only this Picture?

Psychologists refer to 'mind-set' when they explain our persistence in viewing an issue from one perspective. It was a type of mind-set which as a child kept my eyes on the candlestick and not the faces, and we have a mind-set to overcome in our perception of people in other cultures. There is a problem of hunger in the world but it is not due to non-white people being inherently unable to look after themselves. There are processes at work which create poverty, but how do we 'click over' to this other picture, the one hidden in the puzzle?

To see this hidden picture we need to go beyond our immediate response of giving money and to ask whether it is only quirks of nature or frailties of humankind that lead to poverty on this scale. It sounds an easy step to make, but it is not, because built into us is a resistance, a resistance which says:

'It's not my fault that others are poor, so why should I be concerned to do anything more than occasional giving?'

Recently my family and I bought an old and run-down house, and for weeks we had builders, plumbers and electricians working away trying to get it to a habitable state. I got to know the men quite well and during the various tea breaks I could not resist dropping the occasional:

'What's your analysis of the underlying causes of world poverty?' or words to that effect.

They all had opinions:

'Well they're lazy.' 'They don't know how to look after themselves.' 'They must be thick.'

These are not uncommon attitudes – if people are poor it is

5

their own fault. Perhaps it is not surprising that people think this way because we have been brought up with the belief that basically the world works in a fair way and, therefore, when poverty occurs on a massive scale it is either because the people involved need to 'pull up their socks' or it is the result of such unpredictable forces as the weather, volcanic eruption or swarms of locusts.

Yet the world isn't a fair place. Each new born baby doesn't have a clean piece of paper on which to map out its life. If the majority of people in Ethiopia or Bangladesh or Soweto are poor there are very good reasons, and it is not, as my plumber thinks, because their mental processes are inferior to ours. The issues confronting a farmer in the mountains of Ethiopia are much the same as those facing a hill farmer in Wales; an African woman works as hard as a housewife in Tunbridge Wells, and yet their material well-being is grossly different. Different because millions of people are living as if in a giant poker game where certain players not only set the rules but also fix the cards.

To some extent the famine in Ethiopia can be seen as a 'natural disaster'. It is true that the rains failed over a number of years, but equally important were two other terrible factors: a system of land ownership which involved tremendously high farm rents, and civil wars manipulated and fed by an outside power.

The 1985 famine was worse in the northern provinces of Tigray and Wollo. For all of this century these areas have been ruled by the Amhara peoples from which the current Marxist government (and previously Emperor Haile Selassie) draw support. Under Haile Selassie a centuries-old land tenure system by which absentee landlords took anything from half to three-quarters of the farmer's harvest was tightly enforced over these subjected northern provinces. While feudalism was disappearing in most parts of the world, in Ethiopia it was still going strong right up to the overthrow of the Emperor in 1974. Few farmers escaped from poverty. In addition to the high rents harsh taxation was imposed, this being on top of the tithe which the church levied.

Imagine being a farmer under these conditions: at harvest you lose half the crop to the landlord, a quarter in tax to central government, and ten per cent to the church. With such a system

6

it was impossible to build up any reserves that could enable a family to withstand a drought or even a small dislocation of the normal rains.

But Ethiopia is experiencing a double tragedy – drought and war. After generations of being 'sat upon' by Amhara people many of the other national groups, such as the Tigrayans, embarked on a liberation struggle. Like all civil wars these struggles are bloody, but the wars in Ethiopia are protracted because one side – the Ethiopian Government – is being supported by a superpower, and supplied with all the horrible paraphernalia of modern war. The Soviet Union is not primarily supplying the weapons because it particularly likes the Addis Ababa government and thinks their cause is just; it is simply extending its own military and strategic interests. Thus the suffering of millions of peasant farmers is compounded because Ethiopia has become a pawn, albeit a small one, in the struggle for power between West and East.

The poor can pull at their socks as much as they like, with little result, because they are caught in the middle. Unhappily Ethiopia is not unique. The electrician and plumber working in my house don't see the causes of suffering in Africa this way, but why should they? Most of what we learn from television and newspapers doesn't really challenge our fundamental view about how the world ticks.

The Hidden Image

In a distant country there is a factory, a factory making goods which are sold here in Europe, and because they are cheap they sell very well. To produce so cheaply the factory has to cut corners, and one such corner is *safety*. There are no guards on the machines, no money is spent on worker training and no first aid facilities are provided, while the judicious use of 'presents' ensures that the small number of factory inspectors do not interfere with this efficiency. So while the factory is labour cost-effective there are numerous accidents; about one arm a month is severed and fingers are lost almost weekly. Unfortunately the nearest hospital is many miles away and so many of the injuries prove fatal.

A group of Christians living in the local town were shocked by these injuries and decided to do something. They organised the equivalent to our jumble sales and coffee mornings and raised

Civil war in Ethiopia. A woman Tigray People's Liberation Front member helps to load firewood.

Photo : Kirsty Wright – REST

sufficient money to set up a first aid post outside the factory gates. Though the number of injuries remain unchanged the fatalities dropped significantly, and the group was rightly pleased with its efforts.

But then one of the team suggested that perhaps they should do something to prevent the injuries occurring in the first place, in other words set about changing the conditions inside the factory. They could report the manager to the owner of the company, organise the workers to demand safety procedures or march to the town hall and ask for government action. His fellow Christians were horrified at the suggestion. The manager was only doing his job: the factory was in competition with those in other towns and if it were not run efficiently it would be forced to close down. Besides what he was suggesting was 'political' and the Church was not called to be involved in politics. They rejected his idea and continued their work at the gates. They are still there today.

Were those injuries and deaths due to the manager's sinfulness? The manager would argue that if he didn't run the factory along those lines it would close and then the suffering would be even greater for both the workers and their families. What about the owner of the factory? Surely responsibility lies with him? He too would argue that he is forced to compete with other factories not just in his country but in neighbouring ones. There is a desperate need for foreign currency and if he altered the running of his factory without his competitors doing the same, the government would think him mad and see that he was replaced by a more level-headed entrepreneur. So is the government to blame? The politicians would argue that the rules of world trade are set by those in the First World and that is where the blame lies. So where does the buck stop?

Of course each person must take responsibility for his or her own actions but it is naïve to think that we have unlimited choice; society is structured in such a way that it directs and controls the way we act, and the amount of leeway we have in which our decisions take place. This is obvious, though the workmen fixing my house did not place the suffering of the Ethiopians in this context.

Yet if we acknowledge this fact – that individual actions take place in social contexts – we must also acknowledge that just as there is individual sin, so there is sin in the structures of society. This too may be obvious but it is not obvious to the Christians at

9

the factory gate. It was sin in the economic system which led to 'corners being cut' but they do not see this sin as their concern. For them the Church's job is to preach the gospel and give immediate relief; it is not about changing social and political structures.

The forces that maintain poverty are the other picture in the puzzle. It is difficult to see because we have been brought up to have tunnel vision; vision which has ensured that we focus on 'individuals'. For the last two or three centuries Christian teaching has been concerned with personal morality. The Church needed to change hearts and once enough hearts had been changed the world would be a better place. Of course there is always the problem of original sin, the fatal flaw in our make-up which results in selfishness, greed and aggression, and so we must travel along with the 'grain of human nature' and accept that at the society level things will go wrong.

The concept of evil – of sin built into the fabric of society – has been given a back seat. Perhaps we should not be surprised that those who have done well from the way the world works do not want others to examine the ground rules; concentrating on the frailties of the individual is a much safer bet. Thus the Church erected high walls to keep out whole areas of life and labelled them 'no-go' areas. Inside the walls is the safe ground of personal morality and salvation; outside are the marsh lands where messy issues exist such as power, the control of trade, the exploitation of natural resources, the provision of health and education, defence and all the other subjects we call 'political'.

When we look into the Third World puzzle we do not see a picture but a caricature – the Third World has problems, problems which are of their own making, but problems which need our European know-how to solve. Only by searching behind the immediately obvious can we find the real picture. It is a picture of peoples whose culture and talents are as varied as our own but whose material poverty is bound up with our history and our economic and political systems; systems that in many cases we created and continue to support. When it comes to 'us over here' and our understanding of 'them over there' we are in desperate need of a new perspective. We have to move away from the compassion of patrons to the compassion of partners, and this process will start only when we look at the forces keeping a thousand million people at the margin of existence.

10

Factories in Asia, Africa and Latin America are in competition to provide cheap goods for western markets.

Chapter Two

Prodigal Sons

Like the prodigal son it is often claimed that Third World countries have wasted their inheritance, and that this is the real cause of their poverty.

'The poor may have the cards stacked against them but nearly all countries of Africa, Asia, Latin America and the Pacific are now independent and have been for ten or twenty years, so if their people are poor it is their own government's fault, and there's nothing we can do about that.'

Those who say this appear to have a valid point. There are few countries which are not independent, and after twenty years or more of deciding their own futures surely blame for poverty must be placed squarely on the shoulders of the new governments? Of course this argument assumes that everything was fine at the point when these countries became independent, and that since independence they have been free to follow the policies of their own choice. In reality this has rarely been the case. As the old flags were lowered and the new ones hauled aloft people found that the inheritance handed over was not the one they would have chosen.

The 'prodigal son' argument also assumes that by standing back and not interfering we are enabling these Third World countries to work out their own futures. If only this were true! But, in fact, our actions are far from neutral. By covert, and not so covert, manipulations we maintain our interests; we try to ensure that it is our companies and not their rivals which win the trade contracts; we attempt to maintain supplies of cheap raw materials by encouraging Third World governments to produce even more, and as far as possible we see to it that 'friendly' administrations, however unpopular with their own people, remain in power. In other words we are quite prepared to interfere when it is in our own interests to do so, but shake our heads and tell them to 'stand on their own feet' when offering help is not directly to our own advantage.

Far from being independent, the poorest nations of the world are not free to decide their own futures. They are trapped by the legacy of an inappropriate economy; trapped into the

Haitian cane-cuttter. Sugar was one of the main reasons we 'developed' such places as the West Indies.

Photo : Philip Wolmuth

possession of an educational system geared to the past needs of a colonial administration; trapped into being exporters of agricultural products but importers of industrial goods, and trapped into being street vendors in a world economy dominated by superstores. However did they get into such a mess?

Recently I came across a quotation from the writings of the nineteenth century economist, John Stuart Mill. Referring to the reasons we acquired land overseas, he said:

'Our West Indian colonies, for example, cannot be regarded as countries ... The West Indies are a place where England finds it convenient to carry on the production of sugar, coffee and a few other tropical commodities.'

I find the arrogance of that shocking; the people, the land, even the climate are just so many units of production, a place where we find it 'convenient' to grow things we need – a sort of English greenhouse floating a little offshore from Torquay.

The white substance we call sugar was one of the main

13

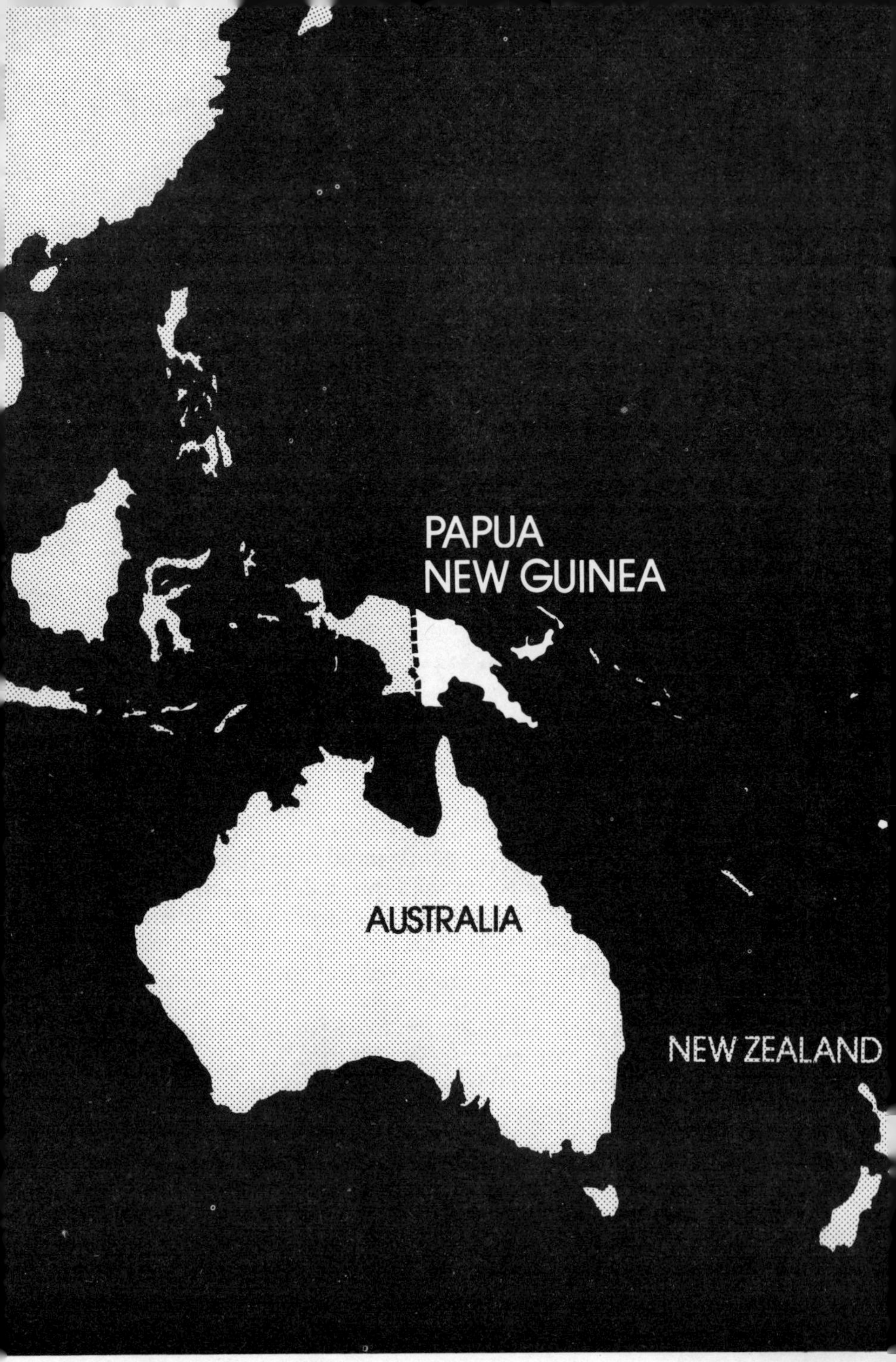
PAPUA
NEW GUINEA
AUSTRALIA
NEW ZEALAND

reasons we 'developed' such places as the West Indies. Today we rightly hold up our hands in horror at the trade in drugs such as heroin and cocaine, and do everything we can to prevent addicts dying at the hands of traffickers. But during the seventeenth and eighteenth centuries more people were dying from sugar than die today from drugs.

The difference, however, is that it was the sugar producer who paid with his or her life, and not the consumer. At the turn of the eighteenth century for every two tons of sugar that crossed the Atlantic one slave died; a hundred years earlier the cost had been even dearer with one slave's death being the cost of each ton. It was the land in the Caribbean and the peoples of West Africa who paid dearly for our love of sweet things.

Look at the commodities in today's shopping bag – how many were grown in Britain? Not tea or coffee, not the cocoa that makes our chocolate, not even the cotton in our clothes nor the thread that holds the bag together. Even the food that with pride we call 'home-produced' – eggs, milk and meat – is likely to be from animals fed to a large extent on oils and grains from the Third World. We have efficiently secured our offshore greenhouses, not just in the Caribbean but throughout the world.

I worked for some years in Papua New Guinea, a group of islands in the Pacific, just north of Australia, and saw for myself the inheritance that a newly independent country had acquired. Why did the Germans, the British and the Australians take an interest in this mountain land? Not because they wished to know these cheerful South Sea islanders but because the fertile soils could grow cocoa, coffee and coconuts, while the interior had gold.

Jet Age Tribesmen

The forces that were at work in Latin America, Africa and much of Asia over a period of two or three centuries arrived very recently in Papua New Guinea. In fact the tribesmen made a jump from the stone-age to the experience of calculators, television, condoms and coca cola in the space of fifty years or less. Because contact with the European was so late the first encounters were well-documented by economists, anthropologists and administrators, and so there is a rare opportunity to see exactly what happened when a Third World people were

Papua New Guinea. A third of the children in PNG suffer from malnutrition.

Photo : UNICEF

unfortunate enough to meet the West. The country was not a Pacific paradise before the European arrived, and it would be foolish of anyone to claim that it was, but there is good evidence that the general nutrition of the people was adequate, and that both the population and traditional systems of agriculture and food collecting were in balance with the environment.

It's not like that now. There are no famines in New Guinea and it is unlikely that we shall see lines of refugee tribesmen crossing over into the neighbouring country of Irian Jaya, but seeds have been sown which are similar to those giving rise to the starvation and suffering in Africa. As yet these seeds have hardly germinated but given another generation or so they may take firm root.

Already the early sproutings can be seen: a third of the children in Papua New Guinea suffer from malnutrition – not acute hunger, but the kind of inadequate diet that leads to poor health, stunted growth and the certainty that the child's potential will never be reached; half the population of three million is under the age of fifteen years and so inevitably the population will double within the next generation; some provinces have a land shortage, and soil erosion and environ-

16

mental deterioration is under way; while in the urban areas there is an almost uncontrollable crime rate as thousands of young people are attracted to the towns only to find unemployment.

Because the tropical environment of the South Pacific is able to absorb abuse and turn the other cheek to a greater extent than is possible in the highlands of Eastern Africa, it is unlikely that we shall see an Ethiopian-type tragedy repeated in PNG, but poverty is increasing and the difference between rich and poor will grow wider unless things are radically changed. To understand how these 'seeds' were sown we need to look at the events of the last two generations.

The country was colonised because it could provide food for our tables and metals for our manufacturers, but labour was needed to grow these crops and to exploit the ore. Thus the native population had to be persuaded to co-operate in these new pursuits. So we took these subsistence farmers and cajoled, squeezed and pushed them into becoming labourers or growing these foreign crops on their own land. A valuable tool in this persuasion process was the head-tax, a tax which had to be paid in cash. The traditional forms of wealth and barter had no value for tax gatherers – only the European-introduced currency would do. So hunters and farmers alike were of necessity forced to take part in the foreign cash economy or face the consequences.

An early photograph taken by a German missionary at the turn of the century shows a priest with a mother who is having her daughter baptised. It was taken on an island where some of the earliest Europeans set foot. When the photograph was taken virtually all the land on that island belonged to the local people. By the time that newly baptised child was ten years old, forty per cent was owned by the white newcomers.

Why did we want the land? Well, we certainly had no intention of growing the traditional food crops. On the island where my family and I lived two-thirds of the fertile land is growing cocoa. Can you imagine a Papua New Guinea tribesman tucked up in bed with a mug of cocoa? Of course not, and they don't eat chocolate either. So there they are, giving over vast areas of their best land to a crop which is virtually useless until exchanged for money. Is there anything wrong with that? Most of us produce goods or provide services for others and

Harvesting oil palm fruits in Papua New Guinea.

Photo : Ray Witlin – IDA

exchange our labour for money, so why shouldn't the people in New Guinea?

The difference is that Third World producers are at the end of the bargaining line when it comes to fixing a fair exchange. So good were we at getting subsistence farmers throughout the world to produce tropical foods and other primary commodities that there is now a buyer's market with the result that the price of these crops and raw materials has not risen in real terms for more than thirty years.

Malnutrition, land pressure and environmental damage are the consequences of the change from being producers of food to producers of export crops. This in itself is a problem but the situation is made worse by the growth of a population set to double within the next quarter century.

'Ah,' I can hear some say, 'they need family planning advice!'

But until they had contact with us their population was in balance with the environment. They practised population control using a range of traditional methods. For example, in many tribal groups the sexes lived in separate houses (the long house) with the women and children in one large hut and the men and older boys in the other village house. Because of this separation the women avoided becoming pregnant for a period of two or three years after the birth of a child. The early Europeans were aghast when they saw this arrangement and learned that husband and wife lived apart.

'We don't live like that in Lower Bavaria (or Chipping Sodbury)!'

How could the family have a loving relationship if they didn't live like us? The system was an anathema to the early missionaries and so, with the best of motives, they set about encouraging the villagers to live in small family groups. They took our advice. The consequences are now coming home to roost and today women frequently have a baby within a year of a previous pregnancy.

Of course this one change, a change which did not affect all the tribes in PNG, is not the only cause for the population increase. Other aspects of their culture and traditional beliefs have also come under pressure. Women had knowledge about plants that could be used to end a pregnancy, while unwanted babies might be left in the forest to die. Not surprisingly, both of these customs were discouraged by the missionaries. At the same time that these social changes were occurring the native population was encountering our technology. The introduction of Western medicine and hygiene dramatically reduced infant mortality with a corresponding effect on population growth. Thus it is not the ignorance or backwardness of the Papua New Guinea people as such that is leading to population increase; for good or ill it is a consequence of contact with our culture and technology.

Independent but Trapped

Countries like Papua New Guinea are now independent but they carry with them a millstone, a millstone called 'the past'. Since the Second World War the agricultural advisory (extension) service, the research stations and colleges, the schools and universities have been geared to an economy which produces for the Western market. It takes many years to establish cocoa and coffee trees, longer still to cajole the culture of once self-supporting people to become earners of cash and buyers of food. But once this policy has been implemented it is even harder to reverse.

Third World countries should be putting food first; that is

A market in the Highlands of Papua New Guinea. The traditional diet was a balanced one.

Photo : UNICEF

implementing policies that ensure they are able to feed their own population. In most countries this could be achieved as the technical problems in producing more are not insurmountable, but in fact it is usually the opposite policy that is being followed. Can it be anything but an evil system which encourages countries like Papua New Guinea with its growing incidence of infant malnutrition, or Ethiopia and Bangladesh with their regular famines, to give consistently more and more resources of money, manpower and effort to growing crops that will be consumed by the obese in the rich world? Surely they should be putting these resources into food production, food that could be eaten by their own people? At best the policies of these Third World governments can be seen as irrational, at worst the result of ignorance, corruption or vested interests. In fact the governments of these countries have little choice but to follow such idiotic policies because they are in desperate need of the income that is earned from exports.

Ironically one of the reasons they need money is to buy food from overseas. Even New Guinea, which had been self-reliant for the previous hundred generations, now imports such things as rice, flour, potatoes, fruit, chickens and beef. In part this shortfall is due to land and labour being used for the production of export crops, in part the imports are to satisfy the needs of the foreign expatriate community, but in part it is the result of both rural and urban people wanting to eat Western kind of foods. After being conquered by another culture it was not surprising that the subjugated people looked to see from where the invaders derived their strength. What the tribesmen saw among other things was polished white rice. New consumer demands were helped along by the foreign companies who held out a picture of the good life; a life where people drink coca cola and smoke Marlboro cigarettes. Today, even in the remotest hill community there is a wooden building – the village store – selling many of the commodities that are commonplace on our supermarket shelves. The transnational companies have been quick to exploit the opportunity, and now that these expectations and aspirations have been established money is needed to satisfy these new wants.

Foreign currency is also a priority at the national level: oil, vehicles, medicines and school equipment are just a few of the items that must be imported. Even if the money were not needed for these kind of goods it is still needed to pay off the country's debts. Papua New Guinea is fortunate compared to many other Third World nations in that its debts are relatively small. Countries like Mexico and Brazil in Latin America or Sudan in Africa have enormous debts, so enormous that the annual repayment of interest can be greater than their yearly income! Imagine what happens if they try to cut back on production of export crops – their creditors very quickly pull them back into line and point out that every bag of coffee and every ton of cotton is needed to service their debt.

Were these countries foolish in borrowing so much? It was the world's bankers in the mid 1970s that put pressure on them to open the financial sluice gates and irrigate their credit-dry economies. Unfortunately the 1980s brought continued recession and commodities fell further so Third World governments needed to borrow even more money just to pay off the interest on existing loans. If ever there was a vicious circle, then this is one.

But what of Aid?

Yet surely aid, that is official government aid from the richer countries to the poorer ones, can offset some of the worst effects of this economic dependency? We think of aid as a 'gift', a generous helping hand, that provides capital for the creation of infrastructure (roads, harbours, power stations etc), that offers investment for new industry and pays for the salaries of expatriate staff involved in training and education. In other words aid is about enabling the economies of these newly independent countries to 'take-off'. Most Third World countries receive quite large sums. In PNG, for example, during the early 1980s, almost half the budget was derived from overseas aid, mainly from Australia. Thus aid is potentially an important factor in assisting Third World economies to stand on their own feet.

Unfortunately, the sad fact is that much official aid does more harm than good. It is not helping Third World countries to 'take off'; on the contrary, it is being used to tie them down, to ensure that they become even more dependent on the World market. Our own government is quite clear as to the purpose of aid. It is given to benefit us. Eighty per cent of British aid, says our

Minister for Overseas Development, comes back to our shores. It returns as tractors purchased, construction contracts completed, and in the salaries of British expatriates. Hopefully some of the money does good in the recipient country, but whether it does or not is incidental. The aim is to extend our interests – commercial, political and strategic. Whether this helps the Third World to reduce poverty is irrelevant.

In the early 1980s Papua New Guinea declared a fishing limit around its coast in an attempt to conserve stocks for use by its own people. The measure was taken prior to establishing a domestic fish canning industry. It was a sensible thing to do. The South Pacific abounds with fish, yet few people, except those living alongside the coast, eat fresh fish, and for most inland families a tin of imported Japanese tuna may be a once fortnightly luxury. Something is wrong when a third of the country's children suffer from malnutrition while there is this great bowl of free protein just waiting to be caught and processed. Setting up a canning factory would at least go some way to improving the nation's diet.

The legislation to establish fishing limits was passed but within days of coming into force a huge United States trawler blatantly operated within a few miles of the coast. The public and the press were in uproar and the navy chugged off to give chase. To the surprise of many they were successful and the offending vessel was brought into harbour. Ten days later the captain appeared in court.

Was the ship confiscated? No. Was the catch confiscated? No. Were the owners fined? No. In fact, not only was the ship let off scot-free, it was given special permission to continue fishing! And why? Because a super-power had made it clear that a little country cannot step on the toes of a big country without facing the consequences, and Papua New Guinea is a recipient of United States aid.

It is hard being a Third World country. It is hard having an economy geared to the needs of people thousands of miles away, and it is even harder when decisions – from the purchase of a tractor to the setting up of a canning factory – can be implemented only so long as they do not hurt those in the First and Second Worlds. The countries of Africa, Latin America and Asia are independent, and have their new flags and national anthems to prove it, but they still have a very long journey to make before they escape from being 'dependent'.

The Prodigal Son wasted his inheritance and suffered accordingly but such wayward action is not the cause of today's poverty in the Third World. By some sleight of hand when these sons came of age, their father cleverly managed to retain the inheritance and to keep them on as labourers.

Chapter Three

Change Things for Good

There is a danger looking into the Third World puzzle; the danger of being overwhelmed by the complexity of what we see. When we believed that poverty was 'their fault', or some perversity of nature, our occasional charitable giving was a sufficient response. But now we perceive the other picture, the one showing people enmeshed in systems, it is difficult to know what actions we can take and far too easy to turn away. Yet there are things we can do, at home, and more directly to support changes within Third World countries.

A practical response, and one that is gaining support, is child sponsorship. It is not surprising that so many people are attracted to this way of helping. A donor in a rich country sends money via a charity to a child or family in a poor country. The money is used to buy clothes and food or, more commonly, to pay for the boy or girl to go through school, while in return the sponsors receive regular letters from the child or reports of their progress. But not all international charities run these schemes and in fact many organisations have reservations about both the ethics and effectiveness of sponsorship.

Those who are worried about sponsorship ask, 'Who is benefitting – the donor or the recipient?' On the face of it child sponsorship, or even whole family sponsorship, seems a good idea, and it certainly appeals to many concerned Christians, hence the rapid growth of such schemes, but is it the best way to help? Is it likely that a child who is poor will have a family that is rich? No, of course not. If a boy or girl is too poor to go to school, too poor to have an adequate diet, too poor to have decent clothing, it is because his or her family are also poor, and in most circumstances the whole community will be poor So, by sponsoring an individual child or family for a few years what is achieved?

A colleague was in Indonesia a short while ago and visited a house where one of the sons was being sponsored by a European. His brothers and sisters were poorly dressed while he had good clothing, they stayed at home during the day while

Children in India. To sponsor or not?

Photo : Max Peberdy

he went to school, they had to cope with the prospect of living in poverty for the foreseeable future, while he was counting the days to his escape to an office job in town. He had become a stranger – an outsider – in his own home, while the condition of his family and the village had hardly changed.

I became convinced that child sponsorship was not the answer during a visit to India. I was being shown around a vocational training institute in Andhra Pradesh where girls were learning sewing and dress-making. At the end of the course they took an exam, and if successful, the qualification enabled them to get a job in the city or start their own business. The college had a high proportion of sponsored students because it needed money and these girls had their fees paid by their foreign parents. Thus sponsored candidates were always welcome even if academically they were borderline applicants. I was introduced to one girl who was obviously very unhappy. She had failed the exam, retaken it, and failed again. When I met her she was preparing to return home to the village.

'Because I have failed in the college I can't get a job now in the town and must go back home. When I was sponsored through school I left my family very young and so haven't learnt the skills a girl must have to be a wife. No village man will want to marry me as I am educated and no good in the house. So what can I do? What have my German parents done to me?'

The intention of sponsorship is to open the door to a better life, but for this girl it had taken her away from her own culture and failed to provide a secure alternative. It wasn't fair to her, it wasn't fair to those left behind and it didn't have the consequences that her German family expected. There are deeply rooted reasons why the people of these communities are poor, so let's try and help the whole community to make the necessary changes rather than provide escape routes for a few individuals, escape routes that often prove illusory. This is an uncomfortable path because to give support to a community necessitates facing the forces at work which keep these communities in poverty. It's not easy, yet it is the only way to bring about long-term change.

Not Poor but Powerless

It is a tautology to say that people are poor because they are materially deprived, but in fact for those of us who do not

27

accept the 'it's all their fault' analysis of poverty this is frequently as far as our alternative explanation extends: if communities are poor it's because they do not have resources; they lack clean water, they lack hospitals, they lack adequate housing, they lack education. The solution is therefore obvious; provide money to dig wells, build clinics, construct houses and staff schools. Well, is this the answer? So long as these resources are provided in response to specific requests of people concerned they are likely to do good, but it is foolish to think that charitable giving can provide sufficient resources to eliminate poverty or even to ensure that there will never be another Ethiopia-type tragedy. It may provide relief, even some short-term develop-ment, but it will not of itself bring the necessary long-term changes. Only by helping the poor to help themselves can poverty be ended, and so the question we should be asking is:

'*Why* do these communities lack resources?'

'*Why* doesn't this village have access to clean water? *Why* are there no clinics or first aid posts in this region of the country? *Why* are there few schools for children living in shanty towns? Is it that they have simply been overlooked? Or is it that for some reason they are consistently missing their fair share of resources?

We use the word 'poor' to describe material deprivation because it is a word understood by all but it has other connotations. We use it in everyday language in a different way to mean 'feeble' or 'pathetic' and thus there is the danger that when we describe people as poor, we convey the impression that they are both materially deprived and incapable of helping themselves. Of course this is the image that many have of Third World peoples but a more accurate description of those living in poverty is 'powerless' because it embodies the cause of their material deprivation.

We saw how the newly independent countries are dependent on Western markets, and while this is true it is not the total explanation for poverty in the Third World. Our hands are not clean of responsibility for this poverty, but neither are the hands of those 'over there'. The type of relationships that exist between the industrialised countries and the Third World nations also exists between the powerful and rich on one hand, and the powerless and poor on the other, within Third World countries (as of course it does in Western and Eastern bloc countries).

28

Not all communities or all sections within a community have equal access to resources. India for example has an affluent business class at one extreme of its social spectrum, and landless labourers hovering above starvation, at the other; in West African towns there are limbless beggars sitting outside each store watching the streams of Mercedes passing along the crowded streets; while in some Latin American countries a mere handful of families own three-quarters of the nation's wealth. It is not an accident that the poor have missed their fair share; it is the rich, some with white skins and some with black, that supervise how the shares are divided.

Which groups of people and which communities are power-less is a result of their unique historical experience, though certain categories throughout the world are frequently in a disadvantaged position. Women in most cultures have far less say in decision-making than do men; minority religious groups usually do badly compared to the majority group; landless people are invariably worse off than those who own land; rural people generally have less clout to influence government policies than does the urban population, and so on.

This latter example can be illustrated from recent events in Papua New Guinea. New Guinea should have a 'food first' policy but such a policy would not be to everyone's benefit. The government took a tentative step to reduce the country's growing love of white rice by cutting rice imports. The idea behind the measure was twofold: first to reduce the amount of money spent on this unnecessary foreign food, and secondly, to boost the income of farmers growing the traditional staple crops. It is accepted wisdom among development economists that if a country is to achieve self-reliance it must encourage farmers to produce more, and providing a profitable and stable market is the best incentive to achieve this. It was an excellent idea, but it didn't work. The import ban lasted less than a month. Why? Because it hurt the people living in towns, and discontented public servants and potential urban rioters have far more power than unorganised and distant farmers. In most Third World countries influence lies in the towns, and govern-ment priorities reflect this fact.

It is a myth that there are not enough resources for everyone to have their needs satisfied. Even the poorest countries have some valuable resources, but certain groups have little or no

Not everyone is allowed to use the public well.

Photo : Max Peberdy

access to what is available. Take water as an example. The charity posters show that in some parts of the world villagers (i.e. women and children) have to walk miles to get an adequate supply. This is obviously wrong and our immediate response is, 'Let's give them money to dig a well or make a dam.' But even when such a resource is available it doesn't necessarily follow that everyone has its use. In India, research in the late 1970s showed that in half the villages surveyed, the Untouchables, that is those at the bottom of the caste system, were not allowed to draw water from the public well. They were not allowed by the caste people because of their 'untouchability'. Such discrimination is against the law, and yet it is a fact experienced every day. Simply providing the money or equipment in these communities does not in itself affect the long-term prospects of the poorest.

Helping the Powerless to Help Themselves

If providing escape routes for individuals is not the solution and even digging wells has its complications is there any hope at all that things can be changed?

In the coastal state of Tamil Nadu in India are many poor villages. To a visitor's inexperienced eyes everyone appears equally poor but in reality there are differences both within and between communities. Some of the inhabitants are traders or landowners and comfortably well off, while towards the bottom of the social scale are the landless and fishermen. In one of the poorest groups of villages, Felix Sugirtharaj is a community worker employed by a voluntary agency called the Association of the Rural Poor. His job is to help improve living conditions; it's a job and a half because these families have been declining further and further into poverty for many generations. At one time many did own a little land, but most of this has gone to the moneylenders and landlords, so all they have left is their skills as fishermen and their strength as labourers. Felix is not a 'doer' but an 'encourager' and 'facilitator', a subtle difference but an important one.

A street light was installed in one of the villages by the local government authority. It was by chance that this village got a light. The main electricity line to the town was erected close by, and it was the council's policy to provide lights for any community alongside the cable. It was a great asset and enabled them to travel around more easily, and to hold their evening meetings at the foot of the post. But then the bulb wore out and was not replaced. It wasn't replaced because no one from the Public Works Department cared whether this village had a light or not. These people were of no importance, had no local politician on the council who would make trouble for the officials, and they had no money to grease the wheels of bureaucracy. So the nights remained gloomy – gloomy that is until Felix was asked to help.

The obvious thing for Felix to do was to travel the fifty kilometres to town, go to the government office, get a bulb and

A meeting in an Indian village.

Photo : Oxfam

return. With his education and air of authority the official would have responded immediately rather than risk trouble, and undoubtedly Felix would have got what he wanted and returned to a hero's welcome. He didn't do that. Instead he encouraged the villagers to call a meeting, in fact a series of meetings, to talk about the problem of the light and why the bulb had not been replaced.

The outcome was that the men travelled to town and went to the office. On the first day the official would not even see a small delegation, let alone allow all the men into his office, so they waited on the verandah, and returned the next day. On the second visit they made it clear that they would stay until he did listen and so the official realised that the best way to rid himself of the nuisance was to give them a bulb. This they accepted, but then sat down again until they received an assurance that in future the light would be maintained. They now have a well-lit village.

Was this cost-effective? No. But it was learning-effective; self-confidence building effective; power to the elbow effective. They had won a struggle, albeit a small one, but one which had

32

started to reverse generations of being at the bottom. They had been entitled to the bulb and learned that together they had the power to exercise that right. This small triumph did not remove their poverty overnight, but they learned that together they had a strength which as individuals they did not possess. Of course it would have been much easier and quicker for the Association for the Rural Poor to have given money to Felix to buy a bulb. That is the gut reaction that most of us have – to put our hand into our pocket and provide the cash for a new well, an ambulance, that child's education, and so on. In some situations this may be the appropriate thing to do, but unless we help these communities to tackle the root causes of their powerless-neess, then those living at the margin of existence will always be with us.

For individuals and communities the daily reality of power-lessness requires them to develop ways of coping with their situation. Often the structures that maintain their poverty have been in effect for decades, and each generation has had to find ways to cushion the knocks. The poor are often described as the 'backward classes', 'fatalistic' and 'lacking achievement motivation', as if it is these attitudes which explain their poverty.

Yet their attitudes are not the causes but the consequences, because how otherwise can one cope with poverty in the face of others' prosperity. Believing in fate is at least one way to handle the pain. But this is not to say the beliefs and attitudes do not contribute to the problem; communities lose self-confidence, they believe themselves to be inferior, and accept that as people they are valueless. It was Felix's job to restore self-respect, and to give back value to their community. The victory with the light was an important step.

Why was it necessary for a voluntary agency to do this work? Governments have extension services, community welfare and social services departments, agricultural colleges etc, so surely only they have the resources to bring about widespread change? In practice for governments to do this, irrespective of their political colour, is a rarity! A rarity because they hold office only so long as they have the support of the powerful, and therefore, their first priority is to maintain the system, because if they don't they no longer remain as the government. The same is true for government workers. For an official, whether an agricultural officer, doctor or health visitor, to support communities in tackling the causes of their powerlessness is to court dismissal or removal to a remote upcountry post.

The relief of poverty is often a stated objective of governments and the usual means chosen to achieve this is 'development', development inevitably being equated with increases in agricultural and industrial production. Most Third World countries place the achievement of development goals high in their priority, and when they decide upon strategy and examine the constraints to development they invariably conclude that what is wrong is 'lack of infrastructure, lack of investment in agriculture, lack of training and education, lack of correct attitudes on the part of peasant producers' and so on.

In other words, like many of us they also see the problem in terms of insufficient resources. This is not surprising because how could a government accept an analysis of poverty in terms of powerlessness when it is the government that is in charge, and supposedly has the ability to change things? Far safer to ignore the real causes and say that poverty is due to insufficient resources, and allow one's stated policy of reducing inequality to become mere rhetoric.

But not only is their analysis of poverty flawed, so too is their way of conducting 'development'. Government departments work to objectives, objectives which are set *not* by the communities they are intended to benefit, but by politicians and civil servants. Thus on the rare occasions when a government worker steps off the main road and visits a village, in his or her briefcase will be ready-made solutions – grow more cocoa, spray the disease on your coffee bushes, borrow money from the national bank, use fertiliser – but rarely are these solutions to the problems experienced daily by the poor.

When Third World governments look into the Third World puzzle they see two pictures – unfortunately they believe that both are valid. They explain the problems of their own economies in terms of powerlessness and the structures that keep poor countries dependent on the richer nations, but when it comes to explaining the poverty within their borders, these urban, well-educated and well-off men see the poor as backward, lazy and lacking drive. Their solution to poverty at home is top-down development where directives are sent to their officials, who as professional persuaders are expected to get the villages and urban poor moving. This way of working is hardly ever successful and so the world is littered with failed rural development projects and urban schemes.

Yet there is hope because there is an alternative; an alternative that we can support. It is change that starts at the bottom; it starts from where the people are and responds to the needs as they feel them. It's not aimed at a temporary alleviation of poverty, but is about enabling people themselves to bring about long-term improvements. It can start with people like Felix being supported by people like us.

Chapter Four

Getting off the Fence

All this may be getting us into deep waters, and it's certainly not what the average person sitting in the pew has in mind when they contribute to organisations such as Oxfam and Christian Aid. In fact it all sounds very 'political', and if there was one thing we learned at our mother's knee it was that religion and politics don't mix. We have usually managed to keep out of these areas in the past, and it doesn't seem right that we should start to imitate politicians.

But Christians are not being called to imitate politicians, in fact that is the last thing we should be doing. Politicians are jugglers; it is in the nature of their profession that they are observers of moods, measurers of temperature and masters of compromise. They are paid to find solutions that will work, to be pragmatic and not too sensitive to the rights and wrongs of any given problem. We are not called to be as politicians but we are called to bring Christ's light into all dimensions of life.

For us to stand back from certain issues is a blasphemy because it is saying that there are realms of creation where God's presence cannot be felt. Our hesitation is the consequence of too narrowly defining the word 'politics'. Popular use confines it to 'party politics' – the business of the Conservative, Labour and Alliance parties, but it should be defined in much broader terms. The Collins English Dictionary, for example, provides the following definition: 'The relationship of men in society, especially those relationships involving authority or power'.

Well, if that is what politics is about, how can Christians avoid being political? After all, the Bible's teaching is concerned with relationships – not only our relationship to God but also our relationship to each other. Yet playing semantic pingpong with definitions doesn't help those who have a genuine unease about individual Christians, or the Church for that matter, being involved in worldly matters. More importantly, for many, it is not being political, as such, which is their worry, but the fact that it involves taking sides, of moving away from the Church as 'reconciler' – of joining hands across divides – and identifying with one group or section of society. The word 'power' is not part of the Christian vocabulary because the Church, at least in the West, has accepted the view that basically life is fair; the earthly fortunes of men and women are in the main determined by their own efforts and that within certain constraints we are free to choose what actions we take.

Thus, in disputes the Church assumes that the central issue is communication, and if the two sides sit down and talk they will resolve their differences and the conflict will be settled. In other words it is not a question of 'right' or 'wrong', just simply misunderstanding, and a reconciler, so long as they remain neutral, can help to bring the sides together. Of course it is true that conflict may occur as the result of misunderstanding; people fail to tell each other things and give or receive incorrect information and in these cases an outside party can help to facilitate communication. However, at other times the cause of conflict is one side's attempt to dominate the other for their own advantage and this has to be changed before any lasting solution can be reached.

Building Bridges from Where?

In some countries Christians are already involved in the politics of poverty. We have only to look to Latin America, South Africa or the Philippines to see clergy and laity as the foci of those committed to bringing about change. How is it that these Christian have moved on from providing 'first-aid posts at factory gates'? Most started their journey from the place we are at now, they too saw the Church's role as being neutral and maintaining a nice balance between opposing interests. Many of these Christian workers came from well-educated and secure backgrounds like ours, but it was the experience of living alongside those in extreme poverty which faced them with the dilemma – to take sides with the poor, or to remain sitting on the fence.

Father Ed de la Torre, a Roman Catholic priest in the Philippines, was faced with just that dilemma, so let us take his road to Damascus. Father Ed has been in and out of prison since 1974. His crime was to help small farmers organise a union, not a criminal act in Britain where the National Farmers Union is a most successful political lobby, but it was considered

Farmers in the Philippines.

Photo : Edwin G Huffman – World Bank

a subversive act in the Philippines. When as a young man he left the seminary, his bishop sent him to a remote village in the hills. As Father Ed trudged up the track on that first day he expected to receive a warm welcome from a friendly, yet respectful community. Imagine his surprise and hurt when he was received with a coolness bordering on hostility. He didn't have to wait long to find out why, as a group of his more vocal parishioners soon put him in the picture:

'You know you priests come to us and preach that we must worship God and go to Church on Sundays; we must not drink

Father Ed de la Torre

Photo : Christian Aid

to excess; we must not gamble; we must not have sex outside marriage; yet such preaching is addressed to our weekends and our nightlife – the periphery of our lives. But from six in the morning until six at night we're in the fields working. We're farmers. So what does the Church have to say about that?'

Father Ed had not been prepared for such a challenge; theological courses are rather weak on such worldly subjects as 'work', 'peasant culture' or 'crop husbandry' and though he could give no reply he thought, 'What a strange question'. But the men went on:

'We are poor farmers who rent our land from the big landlord. He takes most of our harvest and leaves us barely enough to keep our families alive, so we've taken him to court. But when we went to the Bishop and the priests, and asked if

Poor farmers challenged Father Ed to take sides.

Photo : Jenny Matthews – Christian Aid

they would side with us peasants they replied, "Yes, perhaps we should take sides, but that is not our central vocation because we are called to build bridges".'

With a shrug the men turned to Father Ed and asked:

'Have you ever tried to build bridges starting from the middle?'

The following months were a painful period of prayer and reflection, because the priest was being challenged to look at the world from a different perspective, but out of that experience Father Ed realised that just as Christ had identified with the poor, the sick, and the outsiders, he must too. So in their struggle he took sides with the farmers. The cost has been high for the consequence of his decision has been to spend almost a quarter of his life in jail.

Is this story of relevance to us? As a wit remarked about the Anglican Church: 'The trouble with bishops is that generally speaking they tend to be generally speaking.' Well, clerics do talk a lot, but the remark is also aimed at their failure to be specific and to their frequent failure to provide leadership. In other words their expertise is in sitting astride the most precarious of fences. The Church may like to compartmentalise life into areas where it does have a say, and those which are no-go areas, but if only by default, fence-sitting allows the status-quo to continue, and therefore, we are already taking sides – the side of those who are currently having it their way.

How in the face of the daily horrors experienced in places like El Salvador and South Africa, the quiet violence exerted by landlords and money lenders in India and Bangladesh, the manipulation of tribal and national differences by arms dealers, and the daily Calvary of famine-struck Africa, can Christians not take sides? However, to take sides means to take risks; for Father Ed the risk was imprisonment or worse, for us it may mean becoming unpopular among others in our congregation, but for all of us it means facing up to the stark reality that change for a thousand million people cannot be achieved without the powerful losing out. The powerful, whether it be the richer nations in their relationship to the Third World or the élites within the Third World, will not voluntarily give up their ability to sit on the powerless. In the main it is only the poor themselves who can lever them off, but we Christians need to decide on which end of the lever to lend our muscle.

Not Them and Us but We

If we are really to take sides with the poor we need to leave behind the 'us over here' and 'them over there' distinction. This is much harder to do than we might imagine, for just as there exists the stereotype of Africans as all being poor, all pathetic and all passively waiting for us to bail them out of trouble, so we can fall into the danger of romanticising the poor and believing that all are rich in spirit, altruistic and working hard to improve the lot of their fellows.

Well, they are not. The poor are human like us. They are sometimes selfish, they may take advantage of others, if given an opportunity they waste money, and desire self-advancement What we need to remember is that it is the sin in the structures we are siding against. We are not siding with the poor because we recognise them as the nice guys and the rich as the baddies.

41

In Ethiopian art good people are portrayed full-face, while the wicked are in profile. It would be useful if each of us carried such an easily recognisable sign of our characters, but real life isn't like that. Individuals cannot automatically be praised for being poor or blamed for being rich, any more than they are responsible for being born into poverty in Calcutta or for being the son of a Harley Street consultant.

Nevertheless poverty remains a reality. The poor are those who daily experience the consequences of evil in the structures: it is they and not we who are at the margin of existence. Siding with them means taking up their cause and not ours but we can only do this in partnership. I have used the terms 'us over here' and 'them over there' because that is how we frequently speak of the peoples of the Third World, but somehow we have to dismantle this barrier. We shall certainly not do it by going to the other extreme and romanticising the poor and setting them up on pedestals. The peoples of Africa, Latin America and Asia are just like us, and need to be seen as such, 'warts and all'.

The 'warts' may be the hardest part to accept. We can be persuaded to side with the hungry and sick when they are obviously innocent of any baseness, hence the popularity of organisations that deal with children, but extending a hand to sinners has a notoriously bad press. Yet we frequently expect the Third World to be better than us. One of the commonly heard arguments used by supporters of apartheid in South Africa is that 'left to themselves the blacks would be at each other's throats'. The newly independent states of Africa with their inter-tribal disputes are also avidly held up as proof of the inadequacy of the non-whites to rule themselves. The fact that most European nations (and the United States and the USSR) can look back to their own civil wars is conveniently forgotten. We demand that if Third World countries are to have their achievements acknowledged they must first demonstrate their perfection in every dimension of social, economic and administrative life. Until that day they are barred from being considered equals.

Accepting the blemishes is part of our Christian commitment. I recently visited a village in India where some of the young men were being helped to escape from the necessity of going to money lenders. These villagers could not borrow from banks as they had no security and if they were in need, the only option

Young men in India have borrowed money to buy their own cycle rickshaws.

Photo : Max Peberdy

was the local merchants who demanded very high rates of interest. They were landless, and during much of the year there was little work except as cycle rickshaw drivers but the vehicles cost about £90 to buy, a sum far out of reach of these young men. The alternative is to rent a machine from the local rickshaw hirer. However, he takes a very large proportion of the earnings, and so drivers frequently have little to show for their day's work.

In this village a Christian voluntary agency had helped some of the men to borrow sufficient money from a loan fund to buy their own machine and so for the first time they had a real source of income. Once they had broken from poverty there was no holding them back. One man I met had done so well that within a year he had repaid the original loan, and bought a second machine.

'Another rickshaw?' I asked, 'But you can only drive one so what do you do with the other?'

I sensed embarrassment among the officials of the agency as the young man replied:

'I hire it to my neighbours.'

I didn't find out whether he was charging a fair rent or an exorbitant one like the traditional hirers, but it was clear from the reaction of my guides that they feared the 'slave' may have become a 'master'. He didn't feel that he was doing anything wrong; such relationships had been his daily experience, so why shouldn't he do the same?

Unless we accept that people in other countries are like us, and have the same strengths and weaknesses, then we can never hope to enter into partnership. Perhaps of all the difficulties we must face this is the greatest because as we travel from being patrons to partners it is certain that we will experience disappointment, and at times be dispirited by the reversals and failures. Change for good is not easy to achieve, and we must recognise that the poor are mirror images of ourselves. The difference between us is that the social structures that constrain their lives have been expertly constructed to benefit both the rich over there as well as us over here. Once we accept this we can move on from first-aid posts at factory gates and become the Church that sides with those in need.

Chapter Five

Change from Within or Without?

Surely it is going too far to claim that governments in Third World countries only infrequently bring about meaningful change for the poorest of the poor? In fact don't many have a clearly stated policy to improve living conditions?

While it is true that they do have 'statements of intent' they frequently remain just that, statements but little action. If they try to implement change then those who will lose out, be they the moneylenders and landlords in the countryside, the public servants and businessmen in the cities, or a superpower looking for profit from tropical tuna, soon make it clear that enough is enough. Entrenched interests see to it that governments who come to office with a concern for the poor have their manoeuvrability severely curtailed when they attempt to put policy into practice. This is a depressing picture because at first sight it appears that only governments have access to the scale of resources needed to push a thousand million people back from the margin. Even if we accept that the root cause of poverty is the poor's powerlessness, lasting change will surely necessitate not only a radical alteration in relationships but a huge input of money, materials and skills. So what hope is there of this ever occurring if it is only governments that have access to resources on this scale?

The hope lies in the most important resource of all – the people themselves. This is not in short supply but rarely are the reserves of human motivation and talent released to bring about change. The potential has been locked away by the powerful to ensure that the poor remain in their place; systems of land tenure, the exploitation of labour, access to credit, and restrictions in trade and commerce operate in such a way as to benefit the rich. Yet if change is unlikely to come from those that do well from the system, can it be derived from *within* the communities that traditionally have been powerless?

Everyone experiences change as a risk, but for some it is an immense risk; at times it may be a life and death risk. For relatively secure farmers living in the First World to try a new kind of fertiliser or buy the latest piece of equipment contains

Some farm families in PNG have access to education, health and agricultural extension facilities, while others do not.

Photo :Ray Witlin – IDA

an element of uncertainty but only a small one. If the innovation proves a failure then at worst the farmer loses money and the farm income may drop a few percent; his pride may suffer a little but that is all. For most farmers in the Third World to try something new presents a totally different prospect. Fertiliser may cost a thousand rupees a hectare, the precise gain in crop yield can only rarely be calculated, and the possible increase in profit is unsure, but what is certain is that as a share-cropping tenant the peasant will have to give a sizeable amount of any extra yield to the landlord, a man who takes no risk.

The poor are called fatalistic, but in fact they usually make very rational assessments of the risk involved in change and as a consequence are frequently hesitant about new things – better the devil-in-the-system you know, than the one you don't. It is the dangers involved in change, not stupidity or backwardness, which is the basis of their reluctance. But to enable them to use the opportunities that are available, particularly in those situations where the external physical and social environment is rapidly altering, it is often necessary for a 'catalyst' to be present before communities are willing to overcome their hesitation and to organise for change. Felix Sugirtharaj provided that input among those he served. In a similar way to a chemical catalyst he acted as an enabler; not to direct or order, but to respond to needs as experienced by the people themselves.

The development jargon for such a person is a 'change-agent', but when governments use the expression they are referring to officials such as agricultural extension officers, development workers, health visitors, nutritionists, teachers, and community advisors. These officials are rarely 'sons of the area'; often they are only temporary inhabitants as most government workers prefer to reside in the respectable part of town and occasionally visit, rather than live with their clients, in the villages or city slums. Thus they are 'outside' the community, but as part of government they are 'inside' the system, and though they may try to be catalysts, in practice they invariably toss other ingredients into the mixture; ingredients that have been supplied by those who employ them.

Problems? I was on the List

When I worked in Papua New Guinea I was a government employee training rural development officers. Part of the job involved taking trainee advisers on patrol; this consisted of walking to remote villages where we would live with the local people for a week or so to assist them to solve 'relevant' problems. The word 'relevant' is the critical one. The students knew how to prune cocoa trees, treat diseases on coffee bushes, run a meeting and teach farmers a new skill. The idea was that these soon-to-be government advisers would put their theoretical learning into practice on real-life New Guinea guinea-pigs.

Two main tribes live in the province where we held these patrols. The numerically larger one inhabits the fertile and lowland, coastal area. About a century ago the smaller tribe had been pushed up into the hills to farm the poorer land, and so while the lowlanders are relatively well off, the hill tribe are extremely poor with little access to schools, roads or health facilities, and with few opportunities to do anything but farming. It was because they were so badly off that we chose a hill village as the site for one of these patrols. After an exhausting walk we arrived, and following usual advisory practice we asked the

47

**Don't help us to prune coffee and cocoa – we need a road, and a clinic –
that's our problem.**

village big-man (the equivalent of our parish council chairman)
to call a meeting so that we could hear about their problems.
The soil and altitude in the hills is not ideal for growing cocoa,
but as the development of export crops is a government priority
our students had spent a lot of time learning about this crop and
needed to practise their skills. Thus we wanted the farmers to
refer to cocoa as a problem.

'All right farmers,' we said as we sat around the fire that first
evening, 'how can we help you?'

Without hesitation they answered:

'Get the government to build us a road and a clinic, and get
the agricultural officers to come and show us how to grow more
food.'

'No, no,' we replied, 'you don't understand. We want to know
about your problems – what about disease on your cocoa
trees?'

With a disarming simplicity they replied:

'But the government not listening to us is our problem.'

48

CHANGE FROM WITHIN OR WITHOUT?

They were right. The fact that the provincial parliament was run by the lowland people was the reason why nearly all available resources were spent in the coastal areas, and why this village was lucky if it saw a health worker once a month or an agricultural adviser once a year. The lowlanders had a number of political parties representing their interests whereas the highland tribe was trapped in poverty and needed help from outside to catalyse the necessary change.

Did we give that help? No. As a public employee answerable to both national and local government I would have found myself on the next Air Niugini flight home if I had tried to answer their real need. Instead they got a week of cocoa-pruning demonstrations and a slide show on the value of vegetables in the diet!

The problem was not that the local politicians or government ministers were corrupt or any more selfish and shortsighted than the rest of us; in fact the people of Papua New Guinea are fortunate that their culture still retains much of the traditional egalitarian relationships, so that as yet even the difference characterising the richest and most influential nationals do not make them totally distant from village people. It was understandable that the local provincial politicians would ensure that those who had not voted them into office should receive as many of the 'goodies' as were available, while at the national level the government was trying to build a more prosperous society, but as discussed earlier, it was trapped by the need to take into account the interests of groups within the country, and trapped by the world's economy into giving priority to the production of exports.

As an individual I was also in a trap. I had gone to New Guinea expecting to do good, and found that I was part of a system that wasn't answering the needs of the rural people. I was aware of the 'seeds' slowly germinating – child malnutrition, population increase, land shortage, environmental damage, and the drift to the towns. These problems have solutions, but not the ones the government was offering; what I was doing was not sinful in itself, but I was contributing to a policy that was evil. My dilemma was to continue in that system or find an alternative.

What was I to do? Well, fortunately I looked over my shoulder and saw that there were groups attempting to go at least some

49

way towards answering the needs of the rural communities. These groups in Papua New Guinea were, in the main, the church-related voluntary agencies. For example, the Lutherans were running a small training institute for young people to learn how to grow better food crops. It ran short courses, which did not lead to a prestigious qualification as in the state colleges, but provided a practical skill. Also, in contrast to the government colleges the young men and women at the end of the training period returned home to the villages to put their new knowledge into practice whereas the government students became 'white-sock' managers, administrators or advisors in the export crop sector.

Another group were the Anglicans. They had a farm centre which helped local people to increase the protein in their diet by introducing improved breeds of poultry. This would not contribute to the national budget but it was of importance to the health of the farm families. The Roman Catholics provided vocational training in a range of skills that could be used in the village, while the Methodists (United Church) were running an excellent theological college which taught both theology and subjects such as agriculture and health. The students lived in bush material houses and grew their own food, thus when they completed the course the transition back to village life was an easy one. These pastors were expected to return to their people to support them in both spiritual and earthly matters, and that is just what they did.

These agencies had very small budgets compared to government, but they had listened and responded as far as they could to the needs of these rural communities. Of course non-government agencies, not just in Papua New Guinea, but in all countries, are not entirely, or even mainly, outside the political system; they operate within boundaries. Because of these constraints, if any of the church organisations had tried to address the cause of the hill tribe's powerlessness, and helped to organise the campaign at the next local election, or lobby the provincial parliament for a fairer distribution of resources, they too would have run the danger of catching that Air Niugini flight home. Most of these agencies are staffed and funded from overseas; it needed groups established by nationals and run by nationals to bring about radical change.

Non-Government Agencies

Non-government agencies exist in most Third World countries and take many different forms. Some are totally autonomous, while others are the development arms of larger institutions. Their method of working also varies tremendously, partly as a result of their own philosophy or theology, and partly as a result of the constraints imposed by the social and economic situation of the country. Some work in the face of oppressive governments and in extreme danger such as in El Salvador and others are very much in the glare of world publicity like the South African Council of Churches or the development agencies in Ethiopia. Some are entirely secular in constitution; others have a specific religious affiliation and work in communities sharing this faith, while ecumenical bodies may establish agencies with a brief to work among all religious groups. In some parts of the world social change is seen as an integral part of the Christian calling. Many priests in Latin America see no cause to separate the spiritual dimensions of their work from the need to improve the material living standards of their parishioners. Thus very many individuals, and sections of the church, are acting as catalysts.

In Third World countries which maintain very strict controls over the operation of non-government organisations, the agency is often limited to the provision of physical inputs such as money and materials. At the other end of the spectrum are national groups and individuals funded from local resources and these often have greater scope for tackling powerlessness, especially in countries where democratic rights, such as access to courts, are respected.

As a consequence of the various organisational structures, philosophies and situation, different development strategies are followed. Some agencies have a similar approach to government departments; in other words by 'top-down' directives. Aims are created by the organisation and then its field workers persuade or encourage the community to implement the 'plan'. Usually organisations that adopt this strategy have relatively good access to money and personnel and thus can hold out carrots attractive to poor communities.

At the other extreme are those who believe that it should be the people themselves who define goals. In Latin America during the 1970s there was a rapid growth of conscientisation programmes. At the beginning these were organised by individuals – teachers, union leaders, priests and university lecturers – who left their own jobs for short periods to work in the slums or villages. They had few resources except for their own ability as a 'facilitator'. The aim is to restore the self-respect and confidence of people who for so long have been at the bottom. The approach is based on the belief that change can only start once powerless people become aware (or conscious) of their own worth and take action to change their powerlessness. It was from these small beginnings that much groundwork was done for what has become known as liberation theology.

Between the 'top-down' strategy and conscientisation is a range of approaches. Community development is one of the most common. It is built on the concept of being 'non-directive'; a person, such as a social worker, lives with a community, and helps to put into words its problem, and the available options. The precise form of community development depends on how closely associated the organisation is with the power structures such as government.

Whichever approach is taken the criterion of success needs to be 'are these actions weakening the structures that maintain poverty?' It is easy to be fooled into believing that change has occurred. If an agency wants quick, visible results then it adopts the top-down approach; the use of salesman-like persuasion techniques and the provision of hand-outs will almost guarantee visible action – a community hall will be built, a dam constructed, fertiliser applied, mothers take their children to the health clinic – but these actions are the result of outside direction, not the consequence of change from within. The people have reacted by milking resources from the newly arrived cow, but once the outside support is removed, as inevitably it will be, then the community resumes its course under the old system. How could it be otherwise? For nothing really has altered, the power relationships remain intact, and though the community has received some pleasant gifts they have now stopped flowing. It is this approach which has left the world littered with failed development projects.

Change in the structures not only depends on the people themselves changing but also on altered relationships to the groups responsible for the community's powerlessness. To achieve this is a long process. Those who use community development, conscientisation and other non-directive approaches are trying to bring about this kind of meaningful change, but quick results are not possible. This is why governments, even on the rare occasions when they attempt community participation, never think in time-spans long enough to see the work bear fruit; they want results now, not in five, ten or twenty years. However, when change occurs it is sustainable, it doesn't rely solely, or even largely, on the external provision of resources, and even so when the outside agency is no longer present change continues. It was this that Felix Sugirtharaj was attempting to achieve.

But here is a paradox. How is it possible that communities can change from within if they need the help of those who come from without?

The need is for fine judgement; of judging how far an external agency can go in facilitating action without making the community dependent on its support. Perhaps a maritime analogy is helpful here as communities are rather like oysters. Occasionally an oyster is opened and inside is a pearl, something we accept as being of great value. The pearl was made by the oyster but as a consequence of the grit that come from outside. Not all oysters produce pearls, for not all experience that irritant, while others were so overwhelmed by pieces of silt that they died. What is critical is that the agency should know how far to go.

Some non-government organisations have developed the right relationship and these agencies are the channels for our partnership with those in need. Working with these groups we will not become patrons, nor meddlers, and we will not be imposing our ideas about what is good for them 'over there'. Instead we are supporting the changes identified by the powerless themselves. We will not see quick results but we are certainly providing some picks and shovels for the poor to start undermining the constructions keeping them in poverty. There are many signs of hope if we are prepared to look for them, and in the following chapters we will see how such change is occurring in the rural areas of Northern Ethiopia and India.

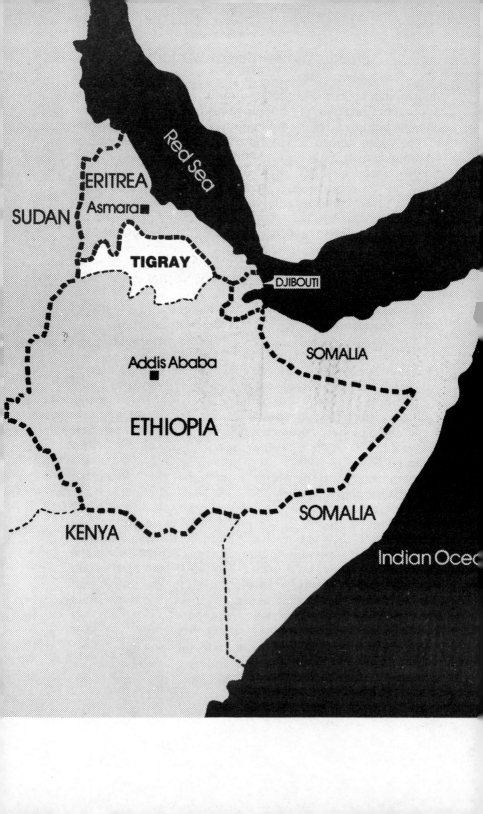

Chapter Six

Partners in Revolution

The old lady looked at the burnt remains of the clinic she had helped to build:

'Oh well, we had planned to make a better one than that even before they destroyed it.'

That is the spirit of Tigray, though it is not the picture we have seen portrayed on television. The media have shown the starvation and suffering in Ethiopia, but with few exceptions the coverage came from those parts controlled by the Ethiopian Government. This chapter looks at what is happening in the famine and war-hit province of Tigray, where 90 per cent of the population live outside the government's control.

Tigray is the most northerly province of Ethiopia, landlocked between Eritrea, Sudan and the province of Wollo to the south. Since 1975 it has been in conflict with the central government. The Tigrayans do not want independence as they consider themselves to be Ethiopians and wish to remain as such, but they want to be part of a new Ethiopia, one in which the kinds of freedom that we take for granted in Britain – the right to elect governing bodies, freedom of expression, access to education and health facilities and so on – are available to all. In other words they want a reconstructed Ethiopia in which all people, both the powerful and the previously powerless, have an effective voice. To us in the West any one living inside Ethiopia is an 'Ethiopian', but in fact there are many different national groups. However, one group, the Shoan Amharas, whose traditional home is the area around Addis Ababa, have held power since the turn of the century. Emperor Haile Selassie was an Amhara, and when he was overthrown in 1974 a Marxist Government came to power, but it too drew its support from this same national group.

For eighty years the people of Tigray have been ruled – oppressed would be a more appropriate word – by the Amharas. It is not a coincidence that the 1985 famine had its severest effect in Tigray, for the Emperor had implemented a policy intended to ensure that Tigrayans would never be a threat to Amhara rule. This policy was poverty. Not just an attempt to maintain material poverty, but also cultural poverty.

In Tigray the people are building and running their own clinics.

The policy worked and 1985 saw the consequences. Under Haile Selassie the policy involved making Amharic the national language and forcibly introducing it into schools and courts. The centuries-old land tenure system by which absentee landlords took anything from half to three-quarters of the peasant's harvest was extended. Under such a system it was impossible to build up any reserves that could enable a family to withstand drought and it forced farmers to cultivate the land in such a way that massive soil erosion resulted. The damage is on such a scale that the province has some of the worst erosion in the entire continent of Africa. But the oppression did not end with these measures. The infrastructure of the province was kept minimal; there was no investment to establish any kind of industry, few roads were built, there were only four poorly equipped hospitals with a total of 300 beds, and three high schools for a population of almost five million. By the 1970s illiteracy ran at 90 per cent and infant mortality at over 50 per cent.

Not primarily a natural disaster but the result of human action – that has to be the verdict on the famine in Tigray. The massive environmental damage resulting from years of neglect means that even in good seasons when the rains fall normally, the subsistence farmers produce barely enough grain to keep their family alive. It needs only a slight shortfall in the rains and the people are pushed over into starvation. The erosion is not the result of ignorance or stupidity on the part of the farmers, but the consequence of injustice. What choice did these powerless people have but to cut down the forests and overgraze the pastures? Allowing the family goat to eat what it could on the slopes too steep to cultivate, and felling trees for firewood to cook the family meal led to erosion, but when you are poor an immediate gain is better than soil in two decades time. Besides, most of the the land did not belong to them and with the average span of life being less than 40 years it was doubtful if many people would be around in a generation's time to appreciate the depth of the landlord's fields.

When the Emperor was overthrown in 1974 the farmers of Tigray expected better things, but it proved an illusory change because the new government, though it had a different political colour, retained many of the prejudices of the old order. There was an initial honeymoon period when the non-Amhara people hoped they would be treated fairly, but it was not to be. Many of the country's national groups decided that the only course was to resist, but faced by the well-armed and Soviet-backed government they felt there was no alternative to an armed struggle. A political and military administration was set up by the Tigrayans called the TPLF – the Tigray People's Liberation Front. The struggle started in 1975 and has been successful, with the vast majority of Tigrayans now living outside the government held areas.

In 1980 the famine began. Each year the rains failed or became less frequent, crops withered and livestock died. At one stage 1,500 Tigrayans were dying each day! In October 1984 the BBC reported and the world became aware of the tragedy though the famine had been inflicting suffering long before it became newsworthy. For most of these years the people of

**The Relief Society of Tigray is responsible for relief and development work
in the areas outside the Ethiopian Government's control.**

Photo : Kirsty Wright – REST

Tigray had borne this suffering alone because the Ethiopian Government gives famine relief only to the towns and rural areas in its control. If help was to come it had to be the result of the provinces's own efforts. In 1978 the people formed a relief and development agency called the Relief Society of Tigray (REST). Initially REST was established to start health and education projects, but as the famine grew worse it took responsibility for co-ordinating relief efforts. From its beginning it has been independent of the military and political organisation within Tigray, and though it works inside the province with the permission and co-operation of the TPLF, its staff, vehicles and money are used strictly for humanitarian purposes.

REST is now responsible for the relief, rehabilitation and development work in the non-government areas. It is running grain convoys from Sudan, arranging the passage of migrants to refugee camps, distributing food in the villages and reception centres, and organising clinics, hospitals and schools. The staff are all from Tigray, many having been teachers or administrators before the war. By the early 1980s it had demonstrated its ability to run large-scale relief operations with efficiency and a number of European and American aid agencies (such as CAFOD, Christian Aid, War on Want and the Red Cross) began to give support.

I was fortunate to spend some time inside Tigray with REST and to experience for myself some of the marvellous things the Tigrayans are doing to help themselves. Let me share some of the things I saw.

Changing things Now

Our vehicle had stopped at the end of a track; before us was yet another dry river-bed, but different from most of the previous ones we had seen in the western lowlands because it had cut its way not through sand, but out of a rocky hillside. We walked for almost an hour along the bed, and then up a barely visible path and into the shelter of some trees. Suddenly the guide held my arm and pulled me back. I was walking over parched earth but we had come to a sudden drop. He smiled at my concern and showed me a safe way down to what I imagined would be the bottom of the cliff, but to my surprise, I found myself facing a door and two windows. What I had taken

59

to be the earthen floor of the wood was in fact the roof of a hospital.

The Tigrayans are masters of camouflage; they have to be to survive. There were seven building, all constructed of timber and built into the side of the hill. After the roof had been made, soil had been thrown on top so that from above it was invisible. The population of this lowland area of western Tigray is one and a half million, but there are only two doctors. A ratio of 1:750,000 is rather more than in the UK where we have one doctor to every 650 people. One of the two doctors was at this hospital. Planning well ahead in Tigray is a necessity if you intend to be seriously ill, as the catchment area is up to a five-day walk.

As I came to know the doctor I realised that he was not a 'doctor' in the sense that we generally understand that word; for us that means a man or woman with five, six or more years training in a medical school, but this Tigrayan had only spent 18 months at a nursing college before the war. However, a few months before my visit a French medical team from the international agency Médicines Sans Frontières had spent just three weeks with him and his staff and given them an on-the-job, in-service training course in surgery; all they needed to know about chopping off badly damaged legs, opening stomachs, and performing a few simple eye operations, in 21 days. And that was just what they were doing. The first building held the surgical ward. There were twelve beds on either side and in one of these was an old lady of 60. She had been blind for the previous five years, but armed with his new skill the doctor had performed one of his first eye operations, and it had been successful. As we entered the ward she could see us, and come over to greet our arrival.

The hospital is run and supplied by REST with money from overseas charities. It cost little to construct as the work was done by the farmers in the region. There are 15 staff and beds for 250 patients. Besides surgery the main work is the treatment of parasitic worms, tuberculosis, malaria, malnutrition and child-birth complications. Part of the hospital's philosophy is that every member of staff must be training someone else, and they have developed a system whereby a student nurse becomes a 'dresser', and then after more training and experience an 'advanced dresser'. But health care is not confined to the

60

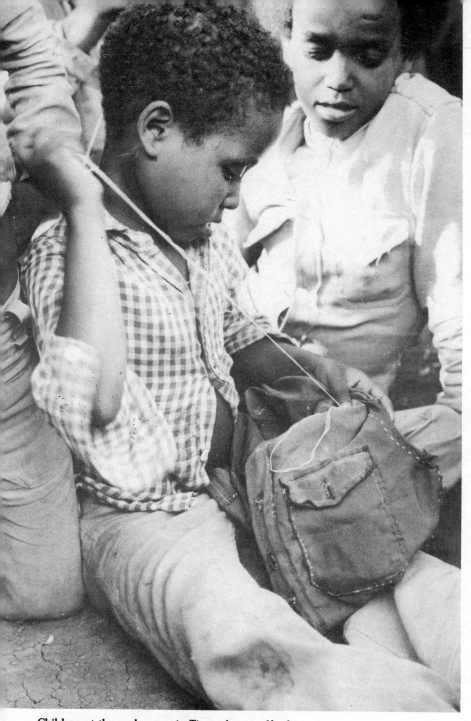

Children at the orphanage in Tigray learn self-reliance.

Photo : Kirsty Wright – REST

Children sleep three to a bed on mud and wood pallets.

Photo : Kirsty Wright – REST

public hospital, and in fact REST have put most of their medical resources into rural clinics.

These clinics are staffed by trained personnel, and are responsible for both treatment and preventative health education among the farming population. I visited a number of them and was impressed by how much was being done with so few resources. Typically a clinic would have the barest of equipment; a cabinet holding medicines all neatly arranged according to use, and a table on which was the record book, up-to-date and showing that the staff were coping with a steady flow of patients. REST is involved in many health programmes, but one of the things it is not teaching is birth control, and they were adamant that people in the West should know the reason for this:

'We cannot teach how to control family size until we have got rid of disease, ignorance and the famine. Then people will be responsive to family planning.'

Too many births is not Tigray's problem, and it is not the cause of the double tragedy they are now experiencing. Children are security. Before the liberation struggle, farmers had little access to either health facilities or education, and REST know that they must demonstrate they can help build a new Tigray, one where the future offers security, before they can ask people to take the risk of limiting the size of their family. Eliminating disease is a tall order but a start has been made. Wherever I travelled I saw groups holding meetings with REST health workers to discuss such topics as the need for latrines and the supply of clean drinking water. The clinics did not belong to REST but to the people, as they had made them. The clinics were vulnerable to attack, both from the air and on the ground, yet far from demoralising the people such action had the opposite result, hence the comment of the old lady recorded at the beginning of the chapter.

As the famine became worse, more families edged towards starvation and so increasingly REST's efforts were directed into relief work. It is REST that organises the convoys from Sudan bringing food and medical supplies. During 1985 and 1986 they were trying to keep alive about half a million people driven down to the lowlands from their mountain villages. REST is responsible for reception camps, feeding centres and orphanages. At one orphanage I visited there were 1,750 children living in bush material houses alongside a small stream. The staff were not only looking after the physical needs of the children, they were also giving them some normality in terms of schooling. There under the trees these children were learning science, history, English, art and even carpentry. Relief work such as this will be a priority for a number of years to come but even amidst famine and war the people are looking to the future: not only looking, but already starting on the changes needed to prevent such a famine occurring again. They are doing this by going to the roots of their past powerlessness. What is happening is a revolution.

Hope amid Disaster

The majority of the Tigrayan population live in the highlands and because of the severely eroded soils it is this area which is most likely to suffer crop failure. Even during normal rainfall years, the families barely maintain subsistence and rarely can they put aside a reserve for use in the bad years. If Tigray is to have a future it must overcome this vulnerability to drought. The way they are approaching this is to take the conventional development approach – the top-down strategy followed by most Third World countries – and turn it on its head. Their starting point is the belief that what has led to the famine is not environmental deterioration, lack of infrastructure, lack of education, the backwardness of peasants or their lack of motivation as such. Their starting point is the injustice built into the fabric of their society. Establish a basically just society and then the rest can be constructed on this sound foundation. This is bottom-up development, where the energy released when farmers have the opportunity to determine their own futures is put into the adoption of a range of innovations relating to social and technological change.

Is it working?

The most important change, and certainly the critical one if long-term agricultural improvements are to be achieved, is land reform. Tigray had a complex land ownership system dating back many centuries.

Traditionally every man was entitled to a piece of land by virtue of belonging to a given community, but the amount of land available to the peasants became progressively smaller. This was partly because the rulers in Addis gave land to their supporters, partly because feudalism forced farmers to sell their holdings for cash to pay for food and taxes, and partly because the destruction of the forests and pastures led to erosion and the subsequent loss of fertile land. By the time Haile Selassie was overthrown a quarter of the families had no land, while almost half of those who did own land had less than one hectare. A small group of powerful landlords held the majority.

Once the liberation struggle was established, land reform was the first important change undertaken by the farmers. Each community elected an agrarian committee consisting of both poor and richer farmers. The first job was for the village to conduct a survey to agree the boundaries, the number of families and the range of soils available. The land was then divided into two categories according to its closeness to the houses and into grades of fertility – fertile, medium and poor – with an agreement as to how much poor land was equivalent to a unit of good land. The criterion for reallocation was the number of mouths the family had to feed. A couple with two children got one unit, those with five to seven, one and a quarter units and so on. It was the community that made the decision, helped by a TPLF member who explained what other villages had done and suggested procedures for conducting the survey and agreeing the allocations.

The change was not without its opponents because a minority of the richer farmers who had done well out of the feudal system were losing out. Through threats and bribery some tried to stop the process, but the opposition was not as great as would have been expected because the big landlords had fled when the Emperor had been overthrown, while the richer farmers were assured that they would not be impoverished as it was only the land that was being distributed, not livestock or implements.

Perhaps more than any other change, this is the one which is the basis of long-term hope in Tigray for now the farmers have an opportunity to improve their situation. They no longer have to give half their crop as rent, and so it is in their interest to farm the land in the best way, to reforest the slopes, and to implement ways of conserving soil and water. This is a firm basis on which to begin making other changes.

'The fingers on our hands are not of equal size because God wanted them to be unequal. Likewise the inequality of man is God-ordained.'

65

A revolutionary picture – a Tigrayan woman learning to plough.

Photo : Kirsty Wright – REST

This was said by a Tigrayan farmer, and traditionally the sentiment would have been echoed by many people. It was not just the poor whose position was explained by reference to God's will, bad luck or their innate inferiority, but also the weakness of women and the minority religious groups such as Muslims. Education is one way that attitudes can be changed, and a climate receptive to new ideas be prepared. With 90 per cent illiteracy, the priority is schools for younger people, and a programme of adult literacy in the villages. The latter are being run mainly by Orthodox Christian priests as they are the largest literate group. Yet attitude has to be accompanied by improvements in the economic and social positions of the powerless groups.

A major step was taken when land was given to all irrespective of religion or sex. Prior to the reform only craft and trade jobs were open to Muslims, while women had been almost totally dependent on their husbands and always had the threat of divorce hanging over them. It is claimed that wife beating is rapidly disappearing as a husband now thinks twice, knowing that if his wife leaves him she will retain her share of the farm. Discrimination against women is grounded deeply in the culture. Though they do most of the physically hard jobs – carrying water, grinding corn, washing, cooking and gardening – in the past they had little say in any of the important family decisions. One job they were not allowed to do, however, was to plough, as it was believed that their inherent inferiority would result in poor cultivation, and a low yield. As one man told me:

'Before the liberation struggle, if my wife had so much as touched my plough I would have thrown it away: she would have so weakened it as to make it useless.'

For this reason enabling women to plough is an important act both economically and symbolically. The TPLF have an agricultural section which is running training courses and hundreds of women have learned the new skill. There is an element of necessity in this change as so many men are involved in the war, or have gone to Sudan in search of work, that in some areas there is no one left but the women. Women want to plough, not because it is yet another job to do, but because it demonstrates more effectively than any slogan their status in the new Tigray. In the words of one woman:

'It's not that clever being able to plough. Anyone can do it. The important thing is that if we learn to plough it means we can learn many other things.'

Because Tigray has some of the worst erosion in Africa, soil and water conservation is essential if the environmental damage is to be reversed. Two main steps need to be taken: first, to replace the trees on the steeper slopes; and secondly to ensure that the rain which does fall doesn't simply run off and away into the Nile but does some good in Tigray. Related to both of these steps is the need to ensure that no more soil is lost. Work is being done by both REST and the agricultural section of the TPLF to identify the appropriate tree species and get planting under way, but greater emphasis is being given to land terracing.

Many different ways of conserving water and soil are being used, but all involve slowing down the rate of run-off from the hills, and directing a controlled flow of water over cultivated terraces. One such site is the valley of Shewata in the highlands where a project was started by the local people in 1983. Large banks have been thrown up using simple hand tools, behind which are strips of land that can be control-flooded when a nearby gully becomes full of water during the periods of short but intense rain. Despite the poor soil, yields on the fist area completed were four times larger than on the surrounding land, and so in 1984 the scheme was extended to 20 hectares, and the following year to over a hundred hectares. The only inputs needed are food and tools and a number of European charities are supporting the work. Local farmers can do the construction but it has to be done outside the growing season. This is the time when the people traditionally leave their homes to look for work elsewhere and so food-support is essential. 'Food for work' schemes are used in many parts of the world and are often criticised, with justification, for undermining local incentive, but in Tigray's circumstances such support is essential. The land reform programme has released the necessary farmer motivation and so it is unlikely that 'food for work' used in this sensitive way, will affect local production. All that is needed is support to get the projects established.

Revolutionary Change

What is happening in Tigray is a revolution – a social revolution. Not merely a change of government, swapping one group of rulers for another, but a change in relationships between people. Land reform, participation in decisions, and access to health and education facilities are the main ways they are trying to achieve change. The energy which these reforms have released is being channelled into development –lasting development from the bottom up; the songs, dances and hopes of mothers, girls, old men and boys, for the first time this century are focussed on change. Their approach to agricultural development will not lead to dependence on export crops, big tractors, pesticides or chemical fertilisers, but to an emphasis on food crops and the use of inputs which are locally available such as manure, terracing and crop rotations. Using simple methods, things that most of the farmers know how to do already but have rarely had the opportunity to implement, the yields of the staple crops can be increased four – or five-fold. Their terrible vulnerability to drought is about to be broken.

Tigray is experiencing a unique set of circumstances, and their approach to change is in response to this situation, but other Third World countries can draw lessons from the Northern Ethiopian experience. Change in Tigray is the result of a partnership: a partnership between the farm families, and the better-educated, politically-aware young Tigrayans who formed the original base of the liberation struggle. As the famine developed, and the need for outside resources became acute, the Relief Society of Trigray became the third element in this partnership. The people of Tigray are united against a common threat, and so many of the traditional differences between Muslims and Christians, landlords and tenants, men and women, have been receptive to change in a way that might not have been possible but for the shared horror of famine and war. The TPLF is not a government but a people's movement. Once the struggle is over and some degree of self-autonomy established in the province, it will no doubt form the basis of the administration and at that point it will be vulnerable to the problems inherent when governments try to implement change. This is a bridge they have yet to cross.

Is there any place in all this for us? Resources are needed: supplies for the convoys, trucks in which to carry the supplies, medicines for the clinics, books and materials for the schools, and food for the families building the terracing schemes. The Tigray people have set the agenda, all they need is help from the outside, and surely that is not too much to ask?

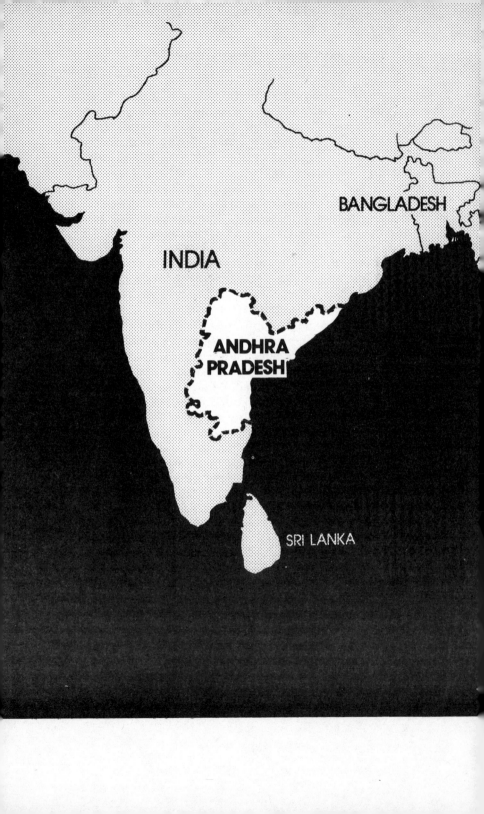

BANGLADESH

INDIA

ANDHRA
PRADESH

SRI LANKA

Chapter Seven

Holding Hands with the Untouchables

India is not on the brink of a social revolution. A country with more than 700 million people and a complexity of culture and history that places our own western civilisation in perspective, is not about to undergo the radical transformation seen in Tigray. India's neighbour may have experienced a revolution, but India is not China. Of course, India has known dramatic events, and in recent history one obvious influence was British rule and the social, economic and administrative changes that were introduced. But filtering India's absorption and adoption of outside influence is her own deeply-rooted culture. The fact that the Hindu religion was old even before Jesus left the carpenter's shop on his journey to Jerusalem, meant that though the sub-continent was given a distinctive lurch, it was difficult to knock off balance even when it experienced the British Raj.

It is a nation of enormous wealth and extreme poverty, but the poor may have more than material deprivation to bear because there is a section of society – the Untouchables – who are regarded as so inherently inferior that they can pollute others. Although these Untouchables are only a small part of the population, about 15 per cent, this is more than one hundred million people, or the equivalent to all of us in Britian and France.

Traditionally the Untouchables performed such jobs as sweeping streets, cleaning gutters, skinning animals and tanning, but today, though some have become teachers, doctors, and even top politicians, most are labourers on farms or in factories. There are many other ways of referring to the Untouchables; Gandhi called them the Harijans or Children of God, while sometimes the word 'outcastes' is used as it is the caste system that is the basis of Untouchability. The caste system is extremely complex, there being four major divisions and more than 2,000 sub-castes. The system relates to all dimensions of life, social, economic, and religious, though the

'Untouchables' perform such jobs as skinning animals, sweeping streets and cleaning gutters.

Photo : Max Peberdy

precise relationship of caste to Untouchability varies from area to area within India.

Legally, Untouchability does not exist; it was abolished by statute in the Constitution. It is an offence to discriminate against Untouchables but those with power – local officials, politicians, landowners, policemen, teachers – are likely to be caste people and so not eager to implement the law, while those Untouchables who are in positions of authority have learnt that survival depends on looking the other way. Discrimination shows itself in many ways. Imagine buying something as simple as a stamp; not a complicated matter for us as we simply go to a post-office, queue for a while and hand over the money. For many Untouchables it is an unknown experience; unknown because their local office may be situated in 'Brahmin Street', a road that only caste people walk along. If Untouchables want to post a letter they must get a low-caste person to make the purchase otherwise they risk being beaten.

India's politicians have their radical rhetoric about helping the poorest of the poor but the fact remains that in many villages throughout the country Untouchables cannot use the local well, worship at the public temple, eat in the town café, be shaved at the barber's shop, or get their clothes cleaned by the washerman. Nationally, more than half the Untouchables (52 percent) are without land compared to only 26 percent among the caste people. Almost three-quarters of Untouchables are in debt, and debt from which it is almost impossible to escape. The practice of bonded labour – of forcing a person to work off their debt – has been illegal since the mid-1970s, but a survey as recently as 1978 estimated that two and a half million people were still in bondage and of those more than sixty per cent were Untouchables. Poverty is not confined to the Untouchables as there are millions of poor among the caste groups, but to be an Untouchable living in poverty is to be powerless in almost every dimension of life.

Sibdavva is married with four children; her husband Ramaiah works for a farmer on the outskirts of a town in northern Andhra Pradesh. They are Untouchables. I was staying in the area with some of the staff of a small Christian agency and being shown their development work among low-caste and Untouchable communities. There was a garden alongside the house where I was living and one evening as I was walking around I looked over the boundary wall into the neighbouring compound. A number of oxen were tethered close to a rice stack and in a corner was a small thatched hut which at first sight I took to be a shelter for the animals, but then I realised that it was someone's house as I could see a woman cooking inside. I was intrigued to know why anyone who could afford a fine walled yard and so many oxen should live in such an inadequate hut, and so when I returned to my host I asked about the people on the other side of the wall. I was told their story.

Of course Sibdavva and Ramaiah didn't own the cattle or the compound, they merely worked for the man who did. They lived in a corner of the yard so they could keep a 24-hour watch on the stock, and getting up in the night to feed the cows was all part of the job. Ramaiah earned about £2 a week; their two eldest boys were also employed by the farmer and received a set of clothes each year and 50p a week, while Sibdavva earned £3 working part of each day in my host's house. Their total weekly income was thus about £6, not much for a 24-hour day, though because Sibdavva was fortunate to have a paid domestic job they were better off than many others in the town. It seemed strange to me that Ramaiah and his sons should work for so little and I asked why they hadn't left this farmer for a better employer. The explanation lay in the family's debts.

A few years previously there had been an election in the town. The farmer whom Ramaiah now works for decided to stand and as he is an intelligent man he hit upon a clever strategy for winning; he would secure the votes of the Untouchables. Though they were only a minority group they still represented a sizeable number of votes and with their support, plus that of a few other groups, he knew his campaign could carry the day. But how to get their support? He went to his friend the bank manager, and together they agreed that the bank would lend money to any Untouchable that wanted to start a business and the farmer would stand as security for the loans. Such arrangements are usually out of reach of the poor and so the Untouchable community knew that the election had sent them good fortune. They quickly took up the offer. The farmer was duly elected and they got their loans. Ramaiah borrowed enough to buy a cycle rickshaw and life was better for a while until he fell ill and didn't have the strength to ride his

Increasingly the rural population is becoming landless. For most working as a labourer is their only employment opportunity.

Photo : Max Peberdy

machine. The family was soon without money but the repayments to the bank still had to be made. The cycle was sold but as few people had enough to buy even a second-hand machine Ramaiah got far less from the sale than he owed. It was at this point that the farmer, now a leading politician, showed just how clever he was, for he visited the family and explained that as the guarantor of the loan he must ensure that it was repaid, and the only way that Ramaiah could do that was to come and work on his farm; the pay would not be very much, but debtors don't have any choice. That was a number of years ago, but the family still owes money, and are likely to for a long time. Ramaiah has no option but to continue working for the farmer, but at least he has an escape route; it is his weekly visit to the cinema and his bottle of toddy. Sibdavva just works.

Rotation not Revolution

Bapathla is a town on the east coast of Andhra Pradesh. In 1977 the region suffered terribly from a cyclone and tidal wave which destroyed houses, flooded farmland, and killed livestock

75

A village on the eastern coast of Andhra Pradesh.

Photo : Max Peberdy

and villagers. A lot of money was given to the region by both the Indian government and Western agencies for reconstruction and one of the non-government organisations that began work in Bapathla and the surrounding villages was CASA – the Churches Auxiliary for Social Action. As the title suggests, CASA is a Christian-based organisation concerned with change, and it employs development staff on projects throughout India. The communities that were affected by the cyclone represent a cross-section of rural life in the region – there were landowners, caste villagers, Untouchables, landless labourers, and fishermen. All had suffered at the hands of this natural disaster but whereas the richer villagers had some reserves from which to rebuild their lives, the poorest became destitute. CASA's aim was to assist the groups most in need, but coming from the outside it was faced by a problem; those who have been at the butt-end of the powerful for generations are suspicious of strangers bearing gifts. Who was CASA? They were offering help, but for whose benefit – the landlords, the moneylenders, the politicians – or more simply, had they come to get conversions to Christianity?

CASA had to demonstrate their good intentions. Using money provided from overseas they began building cyclone shelters. Along the coast they funded the construction of a number of gigantic concrete buildings large enough to house temporarily the population of two or three villages and strong enough to withstand another cyclone. Once that had been done they provided the people with building materials for new houses. These actions had gone some way to relieving immediate hardship and gave security against the danger from a similar occurrence, but they had not affected the basic cause of poverty for these villagers, many of whom lived in identical circumstances to Sibdavva and Ramaiah. However, it was a first step and over a number of years CASA's workers established a relationship of trust.

'It seems a shame,' said Devadas, the CASA project officer, 'that you don't do something with the shelters. Why don't you store things there or use them to hold village meetings?'

He was speaking to the village leaders and as a result of the conversation the buildings began to fill with grain, pots and mats. Then Devadas was approached and asked if he could help in other ways. The people explained that they had little

Devadas is the CASA project officer in this area. A canal runs close by and so the sangum debates whether to get a loan for an irrigation pump.

Photo : Max Peberdy

land, and though many had been woodcutters all the forest had gone and with it their livelihood, so was there any other support CASA could give? Devadas replied that he could help, but only if the community was willing to help itself, as CASA was not in the business of simply providing handouts. He suggested that they use their shelter to hold meetings to discuss their problems, and so it was that a village *sangum* (or association) was started. Many had mixed feelings about joining – some said it was only for the caste people while others claimed it was for the Untouchables – but the meetings continued. At first only men came, but after a few months the women were allowed to attend, and so regularly all the village, both caste and non-caste sat down in one place.

There was no controversy about the basic issue the *sangum* had to face: on that they were all agreed – it was debt and having too few ways of earning money. Once a family becomes poor, especially if they have little or no land, they have few opportunities to build up any reserves of wealth, and when an emergency occurs that requires money, as inevitably it does – illness, unemployment, the expense of a wedding or funeral – then where can the family turn for help? Not to their relatives or neighbours because they are just as poor, and not to banks, as they ask for security. The only source is a traditional money-lender; he will lend, but on what terms? The high rate of interest will be bad enough be he will also demand other conditions; any land they own will become his if they fail to repay and he will need a guarantee from the headman of the village that the community will ensure the family does not default on the agreement. Yet he may demand even more than that. For example, a fisherman who wants money will go to the local fish merchant for a loan. The merchant will lend the sum but insist that all subsequent catches come to him, and him alone; he'll look at the fish, decide which he wants to buy then fix the price! What chance is there that the family will ever escape? Not only are they in debt but their income is mortgaged. The phrase 'poverty trap' is a cliché but how else can this be described? The villagers didn't need CASA to teach them about the causes of never-ending debt, but they did need Devadas to show them ways to by-pass the traditional system of borrowing money.

The answer was a rotating loan fund. It took many months of of discussion but eventually the *sangum* agreed to try the idea

These rich farmers are likely to 'lose out' if the poorer sections of their community become organised.

Photo : Max Peberdy

and a chairman and treasurer were appointed. Each week families saved a small amount and placed it in the fund, often only a few rupees, but with the other sums it soon mounted. CASA helped them to open a bank account, and explained about record keeping and interest. Within a year there was a sizeable amount and this CASA equalled with a loan from their own funds once the *sangum* had shown its ability to manage the savings. When this stage was reached, loans were available to individual *sangum* members. If the economic base of the community was to be strengthened, ways had to be found to earn money and to do this capital was needed. Members were encouraged to propose a project and if the others agreed that it was viable a loan was made at a reasonable rate of interest. Many of the younger men borrowed money to buy cycle rickshaws; one old lady set up a tea-shop alongside the main road to Bapathla; a woodcutter who had lost his job bought

From their own loan fund the people have borrowed money to buy cows, cycle rickshaws, and start small businesses.

Photo : Max Peberdy

materials to make baskets, and many families purchased cows and sold milk in town. What resulted wasn't a revolution and didn't radically alter the situation, but it was a start. For the first time caste and non-caste people, men and women, had sat down together and discussed the reasons for their poverty; for the first time they had acted collectively to improve the situation; and for the first time there was an alternative to ever-increasing debt.

But what next? When I visited the village I sat with them for many hours while they discussed just that issue. Alongside the community is a canal that leads out to sea a few miles distant. There was that fresh water running away to the ocean while in the dry season their fields were desperate for irrigation, irrigation that would produce higher yields and more cash. All that was needed was a pump to raise the water and the construction of channels. The *sangum* was discussing whether

**A puppet show. SPHERE are using many educational techniques to help
the people adopt new approaches to health and hygiene.**

Photo : Max Peberdy

to ask CASA for a loan. To me, an outsider, it didn't seem a very difficult decision, for surely, it was obvious they had nothing to lose by borrowing a relatively small sum, and everything to gain. Yet to my surprise, a heated debate took place. The younger men were eager for the *sangum* to make the application but the older villagers were equally adamant that they shouldn't, and once I understood their reasoning I realised that age and wisdom frequently reside together.

'If we get a pump and start to irrigate our land, how long do you think we will keep the benefit? Perhaps a year, perhaps less. And why? Because the landlords will see to it that the water goes onto their crops, or they'll take the pump away from us. And if that doesn't happen, something even worse will. We have only a little land now, it's only poor land, but at least it belongs to us. Because it is so poor nobody but us is interested in it, yet once it is irrigated it will become good land, valuable land, and the landlords and rich people will want it for themselves. We will lose even the little that we have!

Perhaps we in the West are not very good at perceiving sin-in-the-structures, but for these old men holding their meeting in a cyclone shelter, it was a daily experience. When I left the village they had not resolved their discussion. The younger men argued that things were different now as they had the strength of the *sangum*, and this together with their new sources of income meant they were less vulnerable to the manipulation of the powerful. Who was right only time will show.

Holding Hands Can Damage your Health

Inland from the eastern coast is a town called Gooty, situated in a relatively dry region of Andhra Pradesh. Based in the town is a small independent agency with a long name – the Society for the Promotion of Health, Education and Rural Economy (SPHERE). It is a secular organisation working primarily with Untouchables and has both Christians and Hindus among its staff. They are active in about twenty of the surrounding villages in an area where most of the communities divide into two: the main settlement consisting of the caste people, while a little distance away are the huts of the Untouchables.

Like CASA they have helped to start *sangums* though at this stage the associations have no women or caste people as members. Also like CASA, they had to demonstrate their motives for coming and show that their aim was to support change. They helped build new houses with money allocated by the local government for disadvantaged groups. These grants had been available for some time but Untouchable communities had no access to them because few villagers were sufficiently educated to know how to apply, or rich enough to 'encourage' officials to make available the necessary forms. It could be argued that like Felix Sugirtharaj, the SPHERE workers should have helped the people to do this for themselves, but the agency felt priority lay elsewhere, and that in the face of the people's understandable suspicion it was essential to show SHPERE's ability to provide resources.

Slowly they won the confidence of the communities but it was a hard struggle because though the people accepted that SPHERE's Hindu staff had not come to convert them to Christianity, they could not understand why caste Hindus should want to mix with people like themselves. One of the staff, Kumar, is from a high-caste background and it was his presence that posed particular problems. Normally a caste person would not mix with Untouchables and under no circumstances eat food they had prepared. But Kumar not only drove his motorcycle into their village but sat down and ate with them. It is difficult for us to understand the shock they felt and many would not accept that he was a high-caste person.

'Nobody like that would come here,' they said. 'You are a liar!'

I imagined that he must have been hurt by this reaction; he had gone to help and they had thrown his offer back, and so I asked how he had replied.

'Alright, I am a liar, but if I am a liar you must listen to my words twice as carefully as anyone else, and think about what I say.'

It was a good answer and they came to accept him. SPHERE have helped establish not only *sangums* but also loan funds, village clinics, and the training of local women to be health workers. One of the most interesting aspects of their organisation is the fact that it has been able to draw its staff from such varied backgrounds; not only Kumar but the European wife of an Anglican missionary and an Indian convert to Christianity. How is it possible that these people looked into the Third World puzzle and were able to see that poverty is not simply about lack of resources, but the structures that keep the poor powerless? Why did Kumar, for example, from a privileged town back-ground, whose parents were well-off and had every expectation that their son would have a career and marry a high caste girl, come to be sitting among the Untouchables? I was intrigued to know how he had been able to step outside 3,000 years of Hindu culture and go beyond the expectation of his own upbringing to perceive what so many cannot see. I asked. This is what he told me; whether he intended the story as an objective account of what happened or a modern parable isn't really important.

Kumar was always something of a tearaway at school, and when he went to college he was often in trouble with his tutors, but he had a keen sense of 'right' and 'wrong', and more than anything he could not tolerate hypocrisy, especially hypocrisy among those who held themselves up as leaders. This was why he was angry when a close friend became a follower of a famous guru in the north, because he had heard stories that this wise-man, far from turning his back on worldly pleasures, was secretly a great womaniser. How could his friend be fooled into becoming a follower of such a man?

They were simply rumours spread by the guru's enemies to discredit him, explained the friend, but Kumar decided that there was only one way to protect the gullible from so-called wise-men and so he persuaded his friend to take him to see the guru. It was arranged, and they travelled northwards together but with Kumar giving no hint of his true reason for making the visit. At last they arrived and were shown into the old man's presence, but before Kumar could say or do anything the man said:

'Why have you come here carrying a knife under your clothes that is too blunt even to cut an orange?'

Kumar was shocked because his intention had been to kill, or at least threaten, the guru and he had concealed a knife for that purpose, but before he could reply, the old man got up and led him into the garden.

'You are too weak to hurt me, too weak even to lift up that stone over there.'

Challenged, the youthful Kumar tried, and with difficulty managed to pull it over.

'And what do you see?'

'Only worms,' Kumar replied.

'Then tell me, how is your life different from them? They only eat and reproduce like you, nothing else. What else do you do?' Kumar was so shocked by the experience that he stayed, stayed for three years until finally his family forced him to come home. Without telling him, they arranged a job in an insurance company and did everything they could to get him to conform. But he knew that he must do more with his life than just 'eat and reproduce' and so it was that eventually he found his way to Gooty and work among the Untouchables.

Holding hands with the Untouchables should, like cigarettes, carry a government · health warning, because it can be dangerous. The landowners and moneylenders were not unaware what SPHERE was doing among adjacent communities. They were shrewd enough to read the signs, and events didn't portend well. These traditionally powerless people were beginning to organise, beginning to come together in ways that had not happened before, beginning to save money and start small businesses. If such things continued, where would they find their labour? The landlords were used to women and children coming to their door eager to weed crops, scare birds, carry water or cut firewood, but if they earned money elsewhere, and the children started to attend school, they would not be so eager to work for low wages. The Untouchables were getting above their station and it was obvious who was to blame.

Only infrequently do the powerful voluntarily give up their ability to manipulate the poor but if the powerless are to improve their situation, relations between the rich and poor have to be changed. It was a measure of SPHERE's success that those who were losing out had come to see that the situation was changing, and from their viewpoint, for the worse. As a result there was already one caste village where SPHERE workers could not travel through without receiving abuse, and so alternative routes were being sought which didn't entail passing by the caste houses. The staff knew the risk they were taking, an increasing one if the project became even more successful. They knew the risk because they had read of the riots elsewhere in India, when the 'backward classes' had made gains in jobs and education. Kumar decided that as a high-caste person the worst that would happen to him would be a beating, but for the SPHERE workers who were low-caste or Untouchables themselves, the risk was far greater. It was SPHERE's hope to extend help to the poorer sections in the caste villages and enable them to find ways of improving their situation. In Bapathla, CASA had been successful in bringing together both communities,and it is this kind of action that offers hope that a more just society can be established.

Organisations such as CASA and SPHERE are putting the compassion of partnership into practice. In Britain we raise money, money that is used to dig a well, buy an irrigation pump or finance a loan scheme, and it is right that we should do that, but let's not forget that there are those like Devadas and Kumar whose commitment to partnership is far greater than ours, because they place their lives on the line in order to bring about change.

Chapter Eight

Looking at the World Upside Down

There is an arrogance about our perception of other cultures which for too long has pervaded our relationship with the peoples of the Third World. Rarely have we questioned the assumption that we have much to give, and just as infrequently have we considered whether they have anything to offer us other than the use of their land, labour and climate. When our compassion is aroused, our concern cannot be denied, and the willingness of generations of our most educated and talented young people to work overseas as administrators, teachers and missionaries, is a testimony to that generosity. Yet the kind of relationship that rich countries have with poor countries is not partnershp but one which serves to emphasise the superior positions of those that give. Even at the level of individual Christians, it is the relationship of patronage that we have too readily taken in answering the call to 'feed my lambs, feed my sheep'.

There is a desperate need for a new relationship, one showing greater maturity and one where we accept that we too must be willing to receive. In order to grow into this maturity, we have to go beyond the stereotype of the Third World as a place of problems and apathy. It is this image that dominates our attitudes, thoughts and actions to 'them over there'; think of the black baby posters in our church porches, think of the prayers we offer for the starving, think of the reasons we give to our congregations and neighbours when we want them to raise money, and reflect on how the majority of the world's population is being portrayed.

To accept that other people, other faiths, and other cultures have value even though they are different from what we think of as 'normal', is asking a lot of us, especially at a time when many Christians are demanding 'certainty', seeking an unequivocable doctrine of faith which offers a clear set of rules to follow, and nicely defined boundaries between ourselves and others. To accept that the development of Christianity in Western Europe may not be the only way that God reveals His truth is flying in the face of the security most of us wish to find.

But if we are to journey on the path towards a partnership of equals, we have to recognise that Western Europe's way of ordering the affairs of society and its way to God is not the only route, though this assumption has undermined much of our dealings with others. This is not to argue that all beliefs, values and practices are equally 'good'; they are not and hence we believe that such things as Untouchability and apartheid must be changed. We are called to have discernment, and it is that which has often been absent; the principle we've followed is 'if it's different, it's inferior'. Even today it is difficult to accept the word of this missionary when he says:

'When we approach a person of another culture and of other religions, we have first to lay off our shoes, because the place we enter is holy. Otherwise it could happen that we recklessly destroy the dreams of other people. Moreover, we might forget that God has already been in this place before us. This is not the easy way, but neither is the love of God easy.'

If we had heard and responded to those words a hundred years ago the world would have been a happier place, but we didn't. Instead of removing our shoes we put on boots and trampled over so much. We forced farmers away from subsistence agriculture and twisted and reshaped so much of their tradition and beliefs, not just in Papua New Guinea or Africa, but elsewhere in Asia and Latin America. Of course, it wasn't only we Europeans, or the phenomena of colonisation, that were to blame. Imperialism has never been confined to people with white skins, and throughout history when nations or groups have become powerful they have stamped their culture on the subjugated. What we did was not unique, but the part we played must be recognised: not recognised in order to produce massive feelings of guilt as that would only prevent us undoing past harm, but to make us realise that poverty is not the result of inferiority but the consequence of structures that so often we helped to shape.

Yet the belief, frequently unspoken, but nevertheless present, that poverty is to do with inferiority, is often the foundation of our attitude, and thus for significant sections of the public, eliminating poverty is a lost cause – a situation of no hope. If we are to offset this attitude we must show that there are signs of hope; the partnership between those living in extreme poverty and the men and women working to bring about change is one sign, and there are many others. The vibrancy and joy of

89

Bishop Desmond Tutu of South Africa.

Photo : IDAF

Christ's message being lived out in the churches of the Third World is another. In Britain congregations are dwindling, while in Africa, Latin America and Asia it is a foolish person who arrives late for a service, if they wish to have a place inside the building. How often do we recognise that the most exciting developments in theology are coming from the Third World, or the fact that by the turn of this century the majority of Christians will not have white faces but black ones? If we want signs of hope there are plenty to see.

Bishop Desmond Tutu of South Africa tells the story of the first European settlers in Africa:

'When the white-man arrived,' he says, 'we had the land and he had the Bibles. The white-man taught us to pray and when we opened our eyes we had the Bibles and he had the land.'

It wasn't altogether such a bad deal, for as the bishop goes on to say: 'Perhaps they shouldn't have brought it, because we Africans are taking it seriously,'

Many tribal cultures didn't need scholars to explain the significance of Old Testament concepts such as righteousness and stewardship, because equitable relationships to each other and respect for the environment were important aspects of their existing beliefs. The notion of 'community' and of social obligations to neighbours are key themes in the Bible and yet often they are so foreign to the Western way of thinking that we need to be taught their significance. Our lives centre on 'I' whereas for many non-Europeans the most used pronoun is 'we'. Converts to Christianity in Papua New Guinea may well have less difficulty understanding Jewish history than we do, because some aspects of the ancient agricultural communities of Israel have similarities to their own customs. Take for example the idea of Jubilee – the call to redistribute land and the cancellation of debt; it has parallels in many tribes where land is not owned individually but collectively. Families have the use of certain areas for a period, but once their need diminishes the land is given to those with greater need.

I can be accused here of lapsing into a 'Golden Age' view of times past, of seeing noble savages that have 'fallen' because of contact with us. I am not saying that all was perfect with the Third World until we Europeans arrived on the scene: it wasn't, as given a chance the powerful have always manipulated the powerless. But many traditional customs and practices were

Hector Petersen, the first child to be shot dead by police in Soweto on 16 June 1976.

Photo : Sam Nzima

The quiet dignity of these mothers at a funeral is in stark contrast to the ever-present violence.

Photo : IDAF

closer to the example the Bible has set than our own preoccupation with the individual. We should not romanticise either the past or the poor, but accept that there are things we can learn from both. Yet our perception is so skewed away from this that the balance needs to be redressed. Our congregations need to hear about such people as Felix, Devadas, the leader of the Tigray orphanage, Father Ed, Bishop Tutu and the millions of ordinary people throughout the world who are quietly working to relieve poverty.

Signs of Hope

There is nothing exceptional about Sophie Mazibuko, at least not to look at, as she appears to be an ordinary middle-aged black woman. She lives in South Africa and is the co-director of the Dependents' Conference of the South African Council of Churches. Her job is to support the families of the political prisoners and detainees held under the various laws and emergency regulations. As I say, she doesn't appear very remarkable, and she would not claim to be different from hundreds of black Christians working to bring about change for those living under the apartheid system. Like other blacks she daily experiences the reality of injustice: injustice she faces at

Change is coming.

Photo : IDAF

almost every point in her daily routine; injustice when she travels to work; injustice when she meets with government officials; injustice in the township of Soweto where she lives, and even injustice in her own house – the injustice that stares at her from the eyes of her crippled son.

Television is able to show us some of the terrible events happening in that country, and we feel revulsion at the violence being used by the Government to support the privileges of the white minority, and the violence that is returned by the black inhabitants of the townships. But violence can take many forms – whips, shotguns, armoured 'hippos', tear gas, bombs left in shopping precincts, black policemen hacked to death and burned – these are the obvious reactions to fear and hatred, yet people like Mrs Mazibuko have suffered other forms of violence for many generations.

A few years ago she came to Britain for a short visit and as I was driving her to Windsor to address a church meeting, I asked

94

her to tell me what it was like to be an African under apartheid. Just as she started to reply, we had to stop for some traffic lights.

'Well, I will tell you,' she said. 'Last week I was driving in Johannesburg. Not many blacks have new cars, but I have one which goes with my job. I had to wait at some lights like these, and alongside me stopped an Afrikaner. He lowered his window and shouted, "Hey baboon, where did you steal that from?" That's what it is like to be a black in South Africa. It's the kind of thing we experience every day.'

I felt so angry and ashamed, ashamed at being white. I could imagine the hatred I would feel if just one incident like that ever happened to me. I have never known that kind of abuse or discrimination; only once have I experienced something even vaguely similar. I was on holiday in France and a shopkeeper, recognising that I was a foreigner, served all the local customers before begrudgingly seeing what I wanted. I was very close to showing how he had strained the Anglo-French entente cordiale by breaking a bottle of cheap red wine over his head. Sophie had every reason to hate white people. She is a widow and after her day's work returns home to care for her eldest son. Two years previously he had been shot in the neck by the security forces and now lies paralysed.

She didn't hate. As all who met her found, she had absorbed the hate and then turned it around so that she radiated love. When we look at the bruised, broken bodies of the blacks in Soweto, we see an evil system at work, but we also need to see those, like Sophie Mazibuko, whose life is a response to the suffering of others. The Holy Spirit is at work, not only in South Africa, but among the men and women working inconspicuously in Tigray and India, Papua New Guinea and the Philippines, Latin America and Africa. As westerners we need to hear their stories and extend our hands in order that we can receive. A thousand million people are living in material poverty, but it is we who are spiritually poor in comparison to the vitality shown by Christians in many other parts of the world.

Yet the fact remains that though the Third World has so much to give, it is we who have access to the material resouces which can 'prime' communities to start bending back the structures that maintain powerlessness. But what exactly should our role be in this process of change? Not that of patrons, because that leads to further dependency and increased powerlessness. Should we simply 'leave them alone'? Let them get on with running their own affairs without help or hindrance? I would have sympathy with that view if I believed the First or Second World would leave the Third World alone, or that the powerful within those countries would give space to the powerless, but the likely result is that the powerful would continue to manipulate behind the scenes to ensure that the status quo was maintained.

Looking at the world from a new viewpoint is a start, but where does it lead us? It is interesting to note that in the secular world, opinion is divided as to what the relationship between the First and Third World should be, yet when it comes to the transfer of resources from 'us' to 'them' both the intellectual Right and the intellectual Left are in agreement about one thing – aid is bad.

The Right dislike it because they believe that povery is due to the lack of capacity to produce wealth; create more wealth and though the rich will get richer, sufficient will trickle down to ensure that the basic needs of the poor will get satisfied. This is why aid is an anathema to the Right – it leads to artificial situations where production is supported irrespective of the market, whereas without interference the resources of land, labour and capital would be used efficiently in response to demand. The intellectual Left, on the other hand, believe that poverty is a historical phenomenon. For them, people are made poor primarily as a result of the world's economic system – the weak are dependent on the strong, Third World countries dependent on western markets, the rural areas dependent on the cities. Giving aid strengthens these relationships and bolsters unpopular and corrupt governments; leave these countries alone, says the Left, and once conditions are opportune (or so bad), revolution and structural change will occur.

Invariably, those who propose either of the above arguments are the well-off, well-fed and well-educated, living in secure circumstances; it is their physical security which enables them to hold these opinions, but they are making choices for the thousand million who do not have the option to accept or refuse help from overseas and whose intellectual pursuits are frequently confined to the decisions as to whether to eat their daily bowl of maize flour in the morning or in the evening.

Christ's call is clear; his compassion was not confined to his head but was also of the heart and hands. His response was to heal the sick and feed the hungry, and surely that is what we are called to do. It is right that we provide the soothing cups of water and the first-aid posts at factory gates, because otherwise we are denying that Christ is to be found in those who suffer. Yet we also have been given the gift of intellect, which enables us to perceive how we can extend our help beyond relief and into long-term change.

Partnership, not patronage, is the means to turning the world upside down. We in the richer countries cannot give all the resources needed to eliminate hunger, sickness or homelessness, but we don't have to, because wealth creation is not the primary problem – the big problem is its distribution. Many of the organisations described earlier are enabling the powerless to gain access to the resources which are present in their own countries. Change is coming from within, but it frequently needs an outside catalyst and we can provide some of the resources for that to happen. It may be that giving money is the most effective action we can take, though there are many other measures we can support, and in the following chapter we will look at a range of options. The contribution of the non-government organisations to change is to provide models of what is achieved when people take charge of their own decision-making. Government development agencies rarely work this way, but there are indications that some are now being influenced by this alternative strategy. Our own Overseas Development Administration, for example, is increasingly channelling funds via charities such as Christian Aid and Oxfam, because it recognises that these agencies can reach the poorest in a way that is almost impossible using top-down approaches.

The models that in partnership we can help create are not from the same stable as the models bred by development experts in the 1950s and 1960s, models intended as a panacea for all economic, social and political ills, and that could be taken from one country and released in any other. These were tried and it didn't work. In retrospect the failure is not surprising because each country's problems are the product of a unique set of circumstances and so communities and nations must have the 'space' to make their own mistakes and find their own solutions. The kind of voluntary agencies described here are enabling powerless groups to do just that; to work at the problems of change, and to set their own agenda for escape from the systems that enmesh them. This philosophy *is* transferable from culture to culture, though the form it takes and the outcome of the process will be as varied as the cultural contexts themselves.

We can contribute to these models, these signs of hope. Partnership will necessitate removing our shoes; it will mean looking at the world in a different way and it will also involve us in educating our fellow Christians into the experience of receiving. Finally, this kind of partnership is about recognising the value of others, and looking for the Holy Spirit at work among the powerless; in essence, partnership requires us both to open our eyes and to listen for a change.

Chapter Nine

We Can Do That

'It was a dark and stormy night, rain-heavy clouds swept black fields while hedgerow and tree bent to the northerly wind. Four figures struggled along the water-furrowed track and into the shelter of the wooden hut.'

No, not the opening of a Victorian melodrama but the all too frequent setting for a session on the 'Third World and its Problems'. Getting our congregations out to the village hall on a January evening for a lecture on the famine in Africa may result in a dozen or so stalwarts attending because they 'always support any church function' but it's hardly likely to motivate the community to do anything more than ensure that the Harvest Festival collection goes to Christian Aid and that next year, the hall has an extra night-storage heater. Yet concern for the poor should not be a peripheral interest that intrudes occasionally into 'real' issues of Christian life such as personal morality, remarriage and divorce, or disscusion about forms of liturgy; concern for justice and the right relationships between people is at the core of the Bible and that is why our thoughts, prayers and action about the Third World should be at the centre of our witness.

They are easy words to write but how do we get it into the centre of things? We start by being realistic; Third World issues have as much influence on most of us as the gravitational pull of a distant satellite on the earth, but if we programme the satellite to orbit closer and more frequently then at least we begin to take note of its presence. Similarly with Third World issues, we can have regular times in the Church's year and certain points within our regular worship when we draw attention to the issues and commit ourselves to action. To affect attitudes we must become change-agents within our own communities and like good teachers, that means starting from where people are. In other words, if we are to arouse interest we need to scratch where people itch.

But where does the average pew-sitter itch? Well, increasingly it's likely to be in those areas where the media decide to focus attention. It was television and newspaper coverage that evoked the immense public reaction to Ethiopia, and interest in Band Aid, Live Aid and Sport Aid. Events and people have a reality when the eye of the news-editor falls on them; how many of us would have heard of Mother Teresa, Bishop Tutu, Father Boff, the shooting of coffee pickers in Nicaragua, the rigging of elections in the Philippines, or the coups and counter-coups of African states, without the media? It is our major source of information, often our only source, about events outside our immediate locality, because few of us have the opportunity to travel overseas, to meet non-European visitors or to read books about non-European subjects. The media satisfy our desire for interesting, often sensational news, but rarely make links between events or draw out underlying truths about how the world ticks. We are offered tasty titbits, but these ingredients are rarely blended into a satisfying meal, let alone a banquet. Thus our task as change-agents starts where the media leave off. For example, during the Ethiopian famine, people in Britain were asking, 'Why has it happened?' 'Is this a man-or God-made disaster?' 'What can be done to prevent it happening again?' Doors were opened and the public made receptive to information and debate about these issues. It is at these times that we need to be ready to be provide answers. The phrase that is used to describe this type of activity is 'development education' (though we shouldn't let the jargon put us off).

What are the key isues? Put at their simplest:

Poverty is about being powerless.
Evil structures maintain poverty.
There are signs of hope.
We can both give and receive.

Hearing the issues expressed in such stark terms, we can be forgiven if we reach for the white flag of surrender, for how is it possible to introduce these ideas to people like my plumber and electrician, Major Carter of the Parochial Church Council, Mrs Murray the churchwarden and John Smith with his teenage children, when they repeatedly assert that 'the trouble with them over there is that they're lazy and have too many kids'? Well, we certainly will not do it by getting them together on a cold night in the village hall and hitting them over the head with statistics about the starving, but we may do it if we make Third World issues interesting and relevant, and ensure that words lead to action.

The educational tool that Jesus used was the parable and we can start by following that example. The lives of those working in Ethiopia, India, South Africa etc., provide us with a treasury of material for anecdotes and stories which illustrate both the nature of sin-in-the-structures, and the way that ordinary men and women are bringing about change. Justice and right relationships between people are basic to Christian teaching, but we must not be fooled into thinking that this fact is immediately obvious to our fellow citizens; it isn't, and thus we must introduce these issues with a degree of sensitivity. We should not be over-ambitious in our expectation that Third World issues will automatically appear on the agenda of worship or find regular places in the Church year.

At this stage we need to focus our efforts on certain periods of the calendar and on certain subjects. There are times when congregations accept that hearing about Africa, Asia or Latin America is of relevance – Mission Sunday, Harvest, Christian Aid Week and One World Week are the most obvious, though increasingly other special times are being introduced – Bread Not Bombs Week, Central America Week, Week of Prayer for Christian Unity, and so on.

We can also focus on particular countries or issues. Many churches have links with dioceses in Third World countries or missons where a local person is serving, and this existing interest can be developed.

Agencies such as Oxfam, Christian Aid, and the overseas divisions of our main denominations have development education departments that produce materials and ideas that can support our activities. There are also scores of specific campaigning organisations such as the World Development Movement, Anti-Apartheid, Amnesty International, the Baby Milk Coalition and dozens of Human Rights groups linked to particular countries, that can provide speakers, written materials and channels for action. Importantly, all combine the three key elements – concern; understanding the issues; and practical ways in which we can help.

Of course, there is much groundwork to be done before people with little previous interest in the Third World will commit themselves to doing anything more than placing their usual 50p in a collecting tin, so exactly how do we arouse awareness, then interest, and finally commitment?

Don't beat people over the head with guilt-inducing statistics about world poverty. Emphasise celebration and have fun.

Photo : One World Week

One World Week has some good ideas and guidelines as to how this can be done. The week is organised by the Churches' Committee of the World Development Movement, and over many years the third week in October has seen a range of events initiated, sponsored and locally organised by churches and groups throughout Britain. Its effect has been to sharpen the awareness of thousands of ordinary people and to emphasise the interdependence of ourselves with those in other countries. The key word of the week is 'celebration' – the fact that being part of one world is fun and something that should be joyful. Their experience, often with beginnings in 'cold village halls' but increasingly moving into puppet shows, clowns in shopping centres, curry before communion and riding rickshaws to Downing Street, has enabled them to offer some 'golden rules' as to the ways we should approach events not only during One World Week but at other times of the year.

One World Week's Golden Rules

1 – Know whom you want to involve and make sure you reach them
In other words avoid ending up with twelve cold people in the church annexe! There are three ways of doing this:

(a) Go to where the people are: whenever possible don't organise your own special event but go to where people gather anyway, eg. normal Sunday worship, the public library, a shopping centre.
(b) Get commitment through involvement: people will come if they have a part to play (and parents if their children are involved) so devolve organisation and responsibilities.
(c) Make an offer they can't refuse: present something which is exciting and attractive so that you have to shut the doors on hundreds of disappointed folk clamouring to get in. Selling tickets in advance allows you to test the market.

2 – Get the participants actively involved
A rule of teachers is that we learn by doing. Avoid speaking at people. Even when you have a brilliant preacher, speaker or film, at the very least allow questions or divide into discussion groups. Meeting and talking to an overseas person can be even more effective than the best British speaker or film.

3– Do something new
People need to feel secure and positive about the event but we should still introduce new experiences. It is in this combination of security and novelty that old, hardened attitudes can be changed.

4 – Have fun
Don't beat people over the head with guilt-inducing statistics about world poverty. Emphasise celebration, and the signs of hope.

5 – Know what comes next
The ideal response will be 'Yes, but what can we do?' Have an answer ready.

The rules provide an excellent check list and if followed, one can be fairly confident that a successful event will result. But the goal isn't simply to have an enjoyable experience and raise awareness of the issues; we also need to provide opportunities for practical commitment. As Rule 5 demands – what comes next? Broadly there are four types of action we need to consider – action to raise concern and understanding, action to raise money, action we can take as individuals, and action we can take as citizens.

Action to Raise Concern and Understanding

For development education to be effective it needs to focus, and build upon, people's existing experience. To make the link, for example, between malnutrition in a Third World country and the production of export crops for our tables, why not give free cups of tea outside a supermarket? This can ensure that shoppers stop and think where the commodity came from, under what conditions it was produced and what return the producer received.

An aim of development education is for people to empathise with others, and one of the most powerful ways to enable us to 'step into another's shoes' is to organise a role-play or simulation game. The idea will not immediately appeal to many, especially older people, because it smacks of 'playing the fool' but with careful preparation and explanation, those of all ages can enjoy taking part in an activity where they became a migrant in

Northern Ethiopia, a farmer trying to sell cocoa to a merchant, or a politician in a rich country deciding on trade policy. The reality of power and powerlessness comes home in very dramatic and often unexpected ways.

Worship and prayer take place at all times, though frequently their only non-European concerns have been prayers for those suffering in the world, so include prayers that are not just about the Third World, but have been created by overseas people. Similarly, let's have prayers for those working to bring about change, and use the very joyful and rhythmic songs and hymns from other countries. Few British communities are geographically distant from black churches, so holding joint services and inviting black choirs and preachers is another way we can introduce entirely new and lively dimensions into our often limited horizons.

Remember, get rid of the black baby stereotype; replace it with concern that is blended with signs of hope, and the things we can learn from other people.

Action to Raise Money

Let's not be sniffy about fund raising. There is a tendency for those who come to see powerlessness as the cause of poverty, to move with the force that only converts can muster, to the other side of the pendulum's swing when it comes to raising money. Before their 'conversion', they believed that lack of resources was the cause of poverty, whereas once they accept it is to do with access and distribution, they go to the other extreme and dismiss the need for *any* transfer of resources; from this stems the belief that the only action of value is that which alters our policy towards the Third World. In fact political action and raising money are both needed.

As far as possible, overseas non-government agencies draw financial support from local resources, but because of the nature of their activities and the type of communities they are working with, there is usually a shortage of available local funding. We can give financial support to these organisations directly or via the denominational and secular development charities based in this country. Many churches link their funding to a specific UK organisation and this has the advantage of maintaining the flow of information about Third World issues, and keeping up our interest. It is necessary to remember that not all British charities work in the same way; some have a more traditional relief-type of approach which at times verges on the paternalistic, while others ensure that their relationship is one of partnership.

The public generally gives enthusiastic support to fund-raising but often it is in response to an emergency or request for specific items like an ambulance, bags of food, blankets. But partnership aimed at achieving long-term change requires a long-term and systematic commitment to fund-raising. Giving to the Third World needs to be part of our stewardship of the planet and managed in a similar way to the support we give to our own Church and our own people. To this end, many denominations have introduced schemes whereby churches and individuals can give a regular and set proportion of their income to relieving poverty – one per cent of wages after tax is a popular figure. The money is then channelled via organisations such as Christian Aid, Oxfam and the World Development Movement for both project support overseas and development education here at home.

Ideas about how to raise money are not such a problem. If it's one thing we are good at it's wealth creation.

Action as Individuals

As consumers and producers we have power, though only infrequently have Christian used this power because it is considered to be flirting with the secular and political. But if we accept that politics is about relationships, and that relationships between people are at the root of poverty, how can we avoid supporting or sanctioning products, companies or policies that we believe are assisting evil systems.

No one forces us to purchase a particular country's produce and we can make clear to supermarket managers our reasons for not buying. Similarly, we don't have to place our money in banks, or invest in companies, that are known to be making profits from the suffering of others. However, it may be a good idea to invest a few pounds in the shares of these companies in order to have a voice at their annual general meetings, and a number of concerned groups and individuals have been effective in altering the policy of drug, tobacco and baby-milk companies by this kind of Trojan Horse tactic.

We shake our heads and tut at inter-tribal wars in Africa, but have few qualms as we go off for our day's work in the armaments factory that sells weapons to the Third World. It is big business, and likely to remain so until we as employees and members of the public say clearly, 'This money has blood on it.' But we must accept that for the poor to have a fair deal the powerful will have to lose out, and we are part of the powerful. We must be prepared to see our taxes increase to support the men and women put out of work if our armament companies were forced to cut back on production. Many people may become unemployed, or have to change jobs, if Third World exports increase when our government reduces its manipulation of trade contracts, and as citizens we must be prepared to pay the cost.

There are many other avenues open to us as individuals. The life-style movement based on the philosophy that we should 'live more simply so that others may simply live' is one such route. Another is to support alternative trading companies such as 'Traidcraft', where a range of crafts and good can be brought directly from the producer. This has both a direct economic benefit for Third World communities, and also tremendous educational value for us here.

Action as Citizens

We vote, and that is also power. We can affect events by the way we vote, and also through our ability to influence party and government policies. All the major political parties have sections of their manifestos concerned with aid, trade and foreign relations. As activists we can exert direct influence on what the policy contains, and as citizens we can let politicians know what we think of these policies. If our MP has five letters in a week about a topic, he or she makes a mental note of its importance; twenty letters will cause serious concern. Thus writing to our representatives has a far greater effect than most of us imagine. Twice in the 1980s , the World Development Movement has organised mass lobbies of Parliament – the last one in 1985 saw almost 20,000 people at Westminster registering their concern for Third World issues. Policies will not be altered overnight but we can chip away.

But one thing is vital: if we intend to challenge official policies then let's make sure we understand the issues, and the consequences of our proposals. Opponents of a Christian-based policy towards the Third World will shoot down unsound thinking and woolly proposals. So before we take action we need to work hard to understand the issues. Blindly calling for more overseas aid, irrespective of the conditions attached, is an example of what not to do. Government aid is primarily used to bind poorer nations even closer to the needs of our own economy; what is needed is less of these false gifts, and far more real support directed to the poorest countries, and the poorest sections within these countries. We want 'real aid' not the sort where 80 per cent comes back to us.

These issues are all very broad, and it will be necessary for us as individual citizens to focus on particular aspects in order to achieve results and maintain our own motivation. Joining specific lobbies or action groups is one way of doing this. It doesn't need many people to create a lobby, but their influence on decision-makers can be immense, and often quite out of proportion to the lobby's numerical strength. The forces maintaining current evil systems are huge, so it's time the Christian opposition got its act together.

A Final Word on Action

A few years ago President Nyerere of Tanzania visited Europe, and he was asked what we could do to help his people. No doubt the questioner expected him to answer – send money, or teachers, or trade delegations. But he didn't say any of these things, he simply replied:

'Educate your people.'

President Nyerere was right, for when politicians try to explain why they have policies which far from helping the Third World actually impoverish them further, they fall back on the argument that this is the policy the electorate want. Thinking about my plumber and electrician, Major Carter, Mrs Murray and the Smith family, I suspect the politicians may have been right in the past, but I believe that after the horror of Ethiopia and the public's tremendous response, we are now demanding that as a nation we CHANGE THINGS FOR GOOD.

Chapter Ten

Towards Partnership

A candlestick or two faces? Which picture should we perceive? Must we continue to look into the Third World puzzle and see dehumanised victims of their own inadequacy? Or can we see those black, brown and white-skinned people as valuable, varied and talented as ourselves, although their culture and history have taken a different route from ours? Have we reached that level of acceptance which recognises that difference does not mean inferiority? Because if we are approaching that point, the compassion of patronage that has in the past characterised our charity can grow into a new relationship – that of Christian sharing. It will take much effort to achieve partnership, effort on both sides; on our part we need to erase the starving black baby image; while those who have experienced the butt-end of our arrogance need to heal the years of pain.

We can start by eroding the myth that poverty is the consequence of a thousand million 'individuals' being lazy, backward and lacking motivation. There are good reasons for material deprivation on this scale, and it is not the result of individual sin, but the sin that is built in the very fabric of society. Profit on tins of tuna, chocolate bar sales in our High Streets, and earnings from overseas investments are some of the building blocks that we maintain; while in the Third World systems of land tenure, access to credit, control of commerce, and employment of labour, ensure that the powerless are kept in their place. A new-born child does not begin life with a clean piece of paper on which to map out its course, but for too long the Church's preoccupation with individual morality and salvation has prevented us from seeing what is being done to millions living at the margin of existence. Their poverty is the consequence of the evil present in those no-go areas of life that Christians have labelled 'political'.

Christ's call to love our neighbour means that we cannot ignore the human misery that surrounds us; it is right that we provide the first-aid posts at factory gates, but we have also received the gift of intellect to accompany our compassion, and that gift requires us to go beyond the immediate giving of relief to seeking action that cuts the roots of injustice. We have a choice; on the one hand we can provide resources for individuals; we can believe that they are poor because they lack materials and education, and we can give money to children, families, perhaps even whole villages, to alleviate their poverty. If we follow that course, we build escape tunnels for a few but do nothing to change basic relationships, and as soon as our aid stops flowing, poverty will be re-established. The alternative is to direct our efforts to communities, and to help identify and change the structures maintaining powerlessness. This may be less satisfying for us as we will not see such obvious and immediate results, but when change does take place, it is likely to continue.

Helping individuals is the approach that immediately appeals to us because it is in line with our belief that in this 'fair world', we can all better ourselves by our own efforts. The notion of 'community' sounds altogether vague, and running contrary to our experience of human nature. Yet it is biblically-based, and though it appears an increasingly distant concept to us, in many places of the world it is not an abstract notion but a fact of life, a reality around which social interaction and obligations have meaning.

The word 'partnership' trips very easily from the tongue but it involves a relationship which goes beyond traditional charitable giving – the giving of some of our excess to the worthy poor – to a relationship where we share resources. To enter partnership we have first to accept that others have things to share with us for otherwise it is not partnership but a one-way relationship with inferiors. We need to recognise that what is given is given to benefit the receiver not the donor, and for us in the First World this means leaving behind most of the strings we attach to our support of projects and peoples in the Third World.

In a phrase, the essence of partnership is self-giving love in search of right relationships.

Entering into partnership with powerless communities involves giving support to those bringing about change in the Third World. But how is it possible for change to come from within communities who have experienced powerlessness for generations? And how can outsiders help them to take the risk involved in change, when surely it was outside influence that frequently gave rise to their initial dependency? Won't anything we do simply advance these unjust relationships? The answer to this paradox lies in the nature of the catalysts that facilitate change. The individuals and groups described earlier are enabling communities to restore their self-respect and encouraging the process of education and action. The essence of our partnership lies in support of these catalysts. Rarely are they agents of government, for governments are trapped into supporting the powerful. Hope lies with the non-government, frequently church-related, organisations that have the ability to hear and act upon the needs of the poor.

We in the rich countries cannot provide all the resources to eliminate world poverty, or even ensure that another Ethiopian-like tragedy will not occur again. But the most important resource is already present and that is the people of the Third World themselves. Our primary role is to support them in the 'signs of hope' – the alternative models for achieving change. Government strategies have dismally failed to eliminate, or even alleviate, poverty on any noticeable scale. The world is littered with the evidence of failed development projects.

In contrast our support is for change where the agenda is set and implemented by the people themselves. It is a model that can be reproduced and followed by countless thousands of other communities. It is an alternative to the top-down approach and places emphasis on the process of change – the fact that sustainable change cannot be imposed from above but comes about when people themselves have hope that justice is being built into their society. The energy which this releases can be seen in situations like Tigray, where a social revolution is being carried along in the songs, dances, conversations and labours of both boys and men, young girls and grandmothers, Moslims and Christians alike. These signs of hope exist all over the world. As patrons there is no place for us in this process but as partners, we can share in their joy.

'Educate your people,' said President Nyerere. What is called for is not education in the formal sense of talking at people and filling them with facts and figures about world poverty, but actions aimed at creating a climate of opinion where the people of the Third World are moved from the periphery of our concern into the centre of things. There is little chance that government policies towards aid or trade will radically alter until the decision-makers in Parliament and Whitehall know

111

We can all answer the call to partnership.

Photo : Max Peberdy

that the plight of a thousand million people matters, matters so much that its importance is acknowledged in the party manifestos and election addresses. Such an achievement may seem a long way off but the two major lobbies of Parliament in the 1980s were a beginning and we must not let this initiative falter.

But education needs to draw from people's experience and concern, and for most of us that means those haunting pictures of shrunken-limbed mothers trekking across the Sudanese desert. It is with the problem of hunger, sickness and homelessness that we must begin. Poverty is being old at forty, and dead and forty-five; poverty is having no money to worry about; poverty is about powerlessness. Powerlessness as the cause of poverty is so totally different from the explanation we have been brought up with that it is asking a lot of us to alter our fellow citizen's world view. But hearing about the lives of people like Sophie Mazibuko, Father Ed, Felix, Devadas, and Kumar can change our attitudes where academic analysis cannot.

Their stories also provide the good news from the Third

World; we need to hear about the success stories. Yet if we are to enter into partnership, we must also prepare for the failures. There is a danger that we move from the stereotype of Third World people as all poor, passive and pathetic, to the one where we romanticise the materially deprived because of their poverty. However, so long as we are aware of this pitfall, we are surely justified in turning up the amplifier on the success stories in order to redress generations of bad news.

Finally, there is another danger in looking into the Third World puzzle: we see the problem of poverty, we accept that the causes are evil structures, and we may then conclude that this truth holds only for the people of distant lands. Like someone suffering from long sight, we fail to see that sin-in-the-structures is also to be found in our own society. To perceive injustice as the cause of poverty of them 'over there' but not to draw the same conclusion when we look at racism in Britain, the treatment of three million unemployed, the isolation of our sick and elderly, and the hopelessness that pervades our inner cities, is either the height of hypocrisy or our arrogance insisting that we have nothing to learn from elsewhere. Interest in the Third World must not be allowed to become a soft option that enables us to ignore injustice at home.

The Church cannot maintain those high walls around the no-go areas of life for much longer. Concern for the Third World will of necessity force us to face the reality of the biblical demand for righteousness and justice. The breaches in the wall that Christians in many parts of the world have already made will result, sooner or later, in us challenging the unjust systems that support poverty and discrimination in our own society. In this we share the stuggle to put Christ's teaching into practice and to establish His Kingdom on earth. It is that shared struggle which is the basis of a right relationship with other Christians.

As Lilla Watson, an Aboriginal Australian writes:
'If you have come to help me you are wasting your time.'
But
'If you have come because your liberation is bound up with mine then let us work together.

When we understand and act on her words we will be answering the call to Christian partnership.

FURTHER READING

Theology and Poverty

BOERMA, Conrad
  Rich Man, Poor Man and the Bible, SCM, London, 1979

CCA YOUTH
  Your Will be done, Christian Conference of Asia, Singapore 1231, 1984

CULLINAN, Thomas
  Mine and Thine, Ours and Theirs, Catholic Truth Society, 1979

DICKINSON, Richard D.N.
  Poor, Yet Making Many Rich, World Council of Churches, Geneva, 1983

ELLIOTT, Charles
  Power, Salvation and Suffering, CMS Annual Sermon, London, 1983

ELLIOTT, Charles
  Praying the Kingdom: Towards a Political Spirituality, Darton, Longman and Todd, London, 1985

GRIFFITHS, Brian
  Morality and the Market Place, Hodder and Stoughton, London, 1982

KAIROS DOCUMENT
  Challenge to the Church: A Theological Comment on the Political Crisis in South Africa, CIIR, London, 1985

MEALAND, David L.
  Poverty and Expectation in the Gospels, SPCK, London, 1980

NOLAN, Albert
  Jesus Before Christianity: The Gospel of Liberation, Darton, Longman and Todd, London, 1977

NOLAN, Albert
  The Service of the Poor and Spiritual Growth, CIIR, Justice Papers No. 6, London, 1985

O'GRADY, Ron
  Bread and Freedom: Understanding and Acting on Human Rights, Risk Book Series No. 4, WCC, Geneva, 1979

SHEPPARD, David
  Bias to the Poor, Hodder and Stoughton, London, 1983

SIDER, Ronald J.
  Rich Christians in an Age of Hunger, Hodder and Stoughton, London, 1977

TAYLOR, John V.
  Enough is Enough, SCM, London, 1975

WALLIS, Jim
The Call to Conversion, *Lion Paperback, Tring, 1985*

Natural Disasters

GRAINGER, Alan
Desertification, *International Institute for Environment and Development (Earthscan), London, 1982*

OXFAM
Lessons to be Learned: Drought and Famine in Ethiopia, *1984*

PEBERDY, Max
Tigray: Ethiopia's Untold Story, *REST, London, 1985*

TWOSE, Nigel
Why the Poor Suffer Most: Drought and the Sahel, *Oxfam, 1984*

WIJKMAN, Anders and TIMBERLAKE Lloyd
Natural Disasters: Acts of God or Acts of Man?, *International Institute for Environment and Development (Earthscan), London, 1984*

Food and Development

AID IS NOT ENOUGH
Report of Independent Group on British Aid, *IGBA, 1984*

BUCHANAN, Anne
Food Poverty and Power, *Spokesman, London, 1982*

DINHAM, Barbara and HINES, Colin
Agribusiness in Africa, *Earth Resources Research, London, 1983*

JACKSON, Tony
Against the Grain: The Dilemma of Project Food Aid, *Oxfam, 1982*

HARTMANN, Betsy and BOYCE, James
A Quiet Violence: View from a Bangladesh Village, *Zed Press, London, 1983*

HAYTER, Teresa
The Creation of World Poverty, *Pluto Press, London, 1982*

HOBHOUSE, Henry
Seeds of Change: Five Plants that Transformed Mankind, *Sidgwick and Jackson, London, 1985*

LAPPE, Francis Moore and COLLINS, Joseph
Food First, *Abacus, London, 1982*

REAL AID
Report of Independent Group, *IGBA*

SEN, Amartya
> Poverty and Famines: An Essay on Entitlement and Deprivation, *Clarendon Press, Oxford, 1981*

TIMBERLAKE, Lloyd
> Africa in Crisis: The Causes, the Cures of Environmental Bankruptcy, *International Institute for Environment and Development (Earthscan), London, 1985*

TWOSE, Nigel
> Cultivating Hunger, *Oxfam, 1984*

Development Education

DEVELOPMENT EDUCATION FOR THE CHURCH OF ENGLAND
> General Synod Board for Social Responsibility, *CIO, London, 1983*

LET JUSTICE FLOW
> General Synod Board for Social Responsibility, *Church House Publishing, London, 1986*

MILLWOOD, David
> The Good Samaritans: The Politics of Altruism in Voluntary Aid Agencies, *Lutheran World Federation, Geneva, 1977*

ONE WORLD ON YOUR DOORSTEP
> Planners Handbook for One World Week and Other Events, *One World Week, P O Box 1, London SW9 8BH*

CONTACT ADDRESSES

The following organisations are concerned with Third World issues and development education:-

Anti-Apartheid Movement
13 Mandela St, London NW1 0D0
Telephone: (01) 387 7966

Amnesty International
5 Roberts Pl, Bowling Green Lane,
London EC1 0EJ
Telephone: (01) 251 8371

British Council of Churches (BCC)
2 Eaton Gate,London SW1W 9BL
Telephone: (01) 730 9611

Campaign Against the Arms Trade (CAAT)
5 Caledonian Rd, London N1 9DX
Telephone: (01) 278 1976

Catholic Fund for Overseas Development (CAFOD)
2 Garden Close, Stockwell Rd,
London SW9 9TY
Telephone: (01) 735 9041

Catholic Institute for International Relations (CIIR)
22 Coleman Fields, London N1 7AF
Telephone: (01) 354 0883